This beginner-friendly guide makes learning Google Workspace simple and stress-free. Each feature is explained in clear, everyday language, with easy step-by-step instructions to help you get comfortable with the tools. No technical background? No problem!

Whether you're a student organizing schoolwork, a professional managing projects, or just someone exploring Google's apps for the first time, this book will help you navigate everything with confidence. By the end, you'll know how to work smarter, collaborate better, and make the most of Google Workspace—whether for work, study, or daily tasks.

Table of Contents

PART 1: Getting Started with Google Workspace

Chapter 1: Getting Started with Google Workspace

Google Workspace is a comprehensive suite of cloud-based productivity tools that can streamline your work, boost collaboration, and make managing your personal or business tasks easier than ever. In this chapter, we will explore what Google Workspace is, how it compares to free Google apps, and why it's beneficial for both individuals and organizations. Additionally, we will walk through the process of signing up, navigating the dashboard, and switching between Google tools effortlessly.

What is Google Workspace?

Google Workspace is a collection of productivity and collaboration tools offered by Google, designed to help individuals and organizations work smarter. It includes familiar applications like Gmail, Google Drive, Google Docs, Google Sheets, Google Meet, and more. These tools are all integrated into one platform, providing seamless communication, cloud storage, and document collaboration in real-time. Google Workspace is built to support teams of all sizes, offering robust features for collaboration, file sharing, communication, and productivity enhancement.

Unlike other platforms, Google Workspace leverages the cloud to allow users to access their tools and documents from virtually any device, making it easy to stay connected and productive from anywhere.

Google Workspace vs. Free Google Apps

While Google Workspace shares many apps with the free versions of Google apps (such as Gmail, Google Docs, and Google Drive), the main difference lies in the added features and functionalities designed specifically for business and professional use. Here's a comparison:

- **Google Workspace**:
  - Custom domain email addresses (e.g., yourname@yourbusiness.com)

- o Enhanced security features, such as two-factor authentication (2FA)
- o Google Meet with advanced video conferencing features
- o More cloud storage per user
- o Advanced collaboration tools, such as shared calendars and team drives
- o Admin controls for managing users and security settings
- o Priority support from Google's customer service
- **Free Google Apps**:
  - o Personal Gmail accounts (e.g., yourname@gmail.com)
  - o Limited cloud storage on Google Drive (15GB free)
  - o Basic collaboration tools with fewer options for businesses
  - o Limited support options (community forums and self-help)

Conclusion: Google Workspace provides professional-grade features with enhanced security, custom branding, and scalable solutions that are ideal for teams, businesses, and anyone seeking an all-in-one collaboration hub.

Benefits of Google Workspace for Individuals & Businesses

Google Workspace offers a wide range of benefits that can enhance productivity, streamline work processes, and boost team collaboration. Whether you're a solo entrepreneur or part of a large organization, the platform can help you achieve your goals. Here are some key benefits:

- **Seamless Collaboration**: Google Workspace allows multiple users to work on the same document, spreadsheet, or presentation in real-time. With features like Google Docs, Sheets, and Slides, you can make edits simultaneously with colleagues, ensuring everyone stays up-to-date.
- **Cloud Storage & File Sharing**: Google Drive provides cloud storage, making it easy to store, share, and access your files from anywhere. You can organize your files into folders and easily share them with colleagues or clients with specific access permissions.

- **Integrated Communication**: With Gmail, Google Meet, and Google Chat, you have multiple ways to communicate with your team, whether through email, instant messaging, or video conferencing.
- **Security**: Google Workspace offers enterprise-grade security, including data encryption, custom access controls, and advanced security features to ensure that your data remains protected.
- **Customization**: For businesses, Google Workspace offers custom domain email, branding options, and administrative controls to tailor the workspace to meet your organization's needs.
- **Increased Productivity**: With powerful integrations between apps like Google Calendar, Google Tasks, and Google Keep, you can streamline your workflow, track your schedule, and manage tasks effortlessly.

Subscription Plans & Pricing Explained

Google Workspace offers different subscription plans to suit various needs, whether you're a solo professional or a large enterprise. Here's an overview of the pricing options:

1. **Business Starter**:
   - Price: $6 per user/month
   - Features: Custom email addresses, 30GB cloud storage per user, video meetings for up to 100 participants, and more.
2. **Business Standard**:
   - Price: $12 per user/month
   - Features: Everything in the Business Starter plan, plus 2TB cloud storage per user, enhanced video meeting capabilities, and additional administrative tools.
3. **Business Plus**:
   - Price: $18 per user/month
   - Features: Everything in the Business Standard plan, plus 5TB cloud storage per user, advanced security and compliance tools, and enhanced Google Meet features.
4. **Enterprise**:

- o Price: Custom pricing
- o Features: Unlimited storage, enhanced security and compliance, advanced admin controls, and additional business tools.

Note: Google Workspace offers a 14-day free trial, allowing you to explore all features before committing to a paid plan. Pricing can vary depending on your region and specific needs.

Signing Up for Google Workspace (Step-by-Step)

Setting up your Google Workspace account is easy and takes just a few minutes. Follow this step-by-step guide to get started:

1. **Visit the Google Workspace Website**: Go to Google Workspace and click on the "Get Started" button.

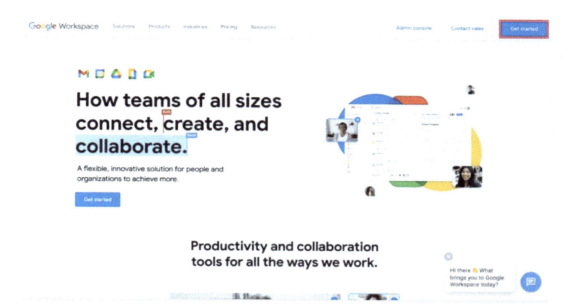

2. **Enter Your Information**: You will be asked to enter your business name, the number of employees (or choose "I'm a sole proprietor" if applicable), and your country.

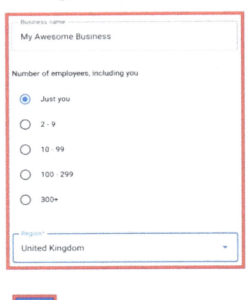

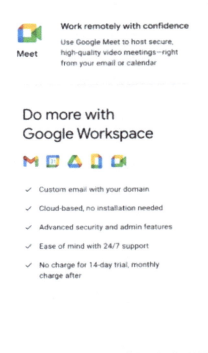

3. **Create Your Account**: Provide your first and last name, as well as your contact email address. Then, you'll need to create a username and password for your Google Workspace account.
4. **Choose a Domain**: If you don't already have a domain, you can purchase one directly through Google. If you have an existing domain, you can link it to Google Workspace to create professional email addresses.
5. **Payment Details**: Enter your payment details to begin the subscription for the plan you've selected.
6. **Complete the Setup**: After completing the payment, follow the on-screen prompts to finalize your setup. You'll be able to access the admin console and start managing your account.

Exploring the Google Workspace Dashboard

The **Google Workspace Admin Console** is where you manage users, settings, security, and billing for your Google Workspace account. It's an essential tool for businesses to configure the workspace environment.

Key features of the dashboard:

- **User Management**: Add, remove, or manage users in your organization including creating custom roles and setting permissions.
- **Security Settings**: Configure security features such as two-factor authentication and data loss prevention.
- **Billing**: Manage your subscription and payment details.
- **Reports & Monitoring**: View activity reports and track usage within your organization.

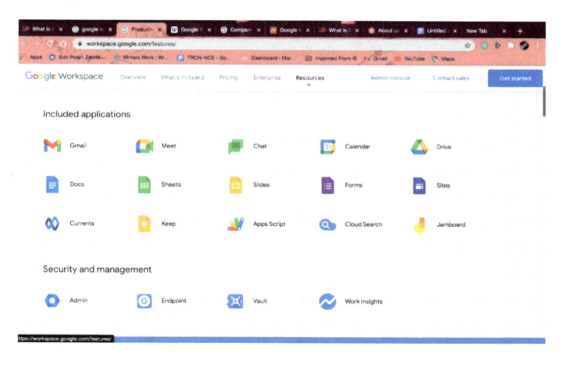

How to Access & Switch Between Google Tools

Google Workspace integrates several tools under one umbrella, making it easy to switch between them seamlessly. Here's how you can access and move between the tools:

- **Accessing Google Tools**: From any Google Workspace app, you can click on the **App Launcher** (the nine-dot grid icon in the upper right corner) to quickly access Gmail, Drive, Docs, Sheets, Meet, and more.

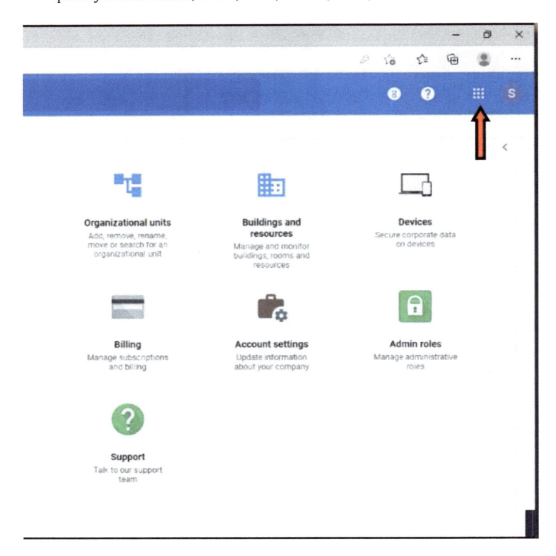

- **Switching Between Apps**: Once you're in one Google tool, simply open the App Launcher to switch to another app without needing to log in again.

💡 *Tip: Use Google Chrome for a smoother experience, as it's optimized for Google Workspace apps and allows you to open multiple tools in different tabs.*

Conclusion

This chapter has provided a comprehensive overview of Google Workspace, including what it is, how it compares to free Google apps, its benefits for individuals and businesses, subscription details, and how to sign up and navigate the dashboard. As you move forward, understanding the fundamentals of Google Workspace will help you make the most of its powerful tools and features, whether for personal use or within your organization.

Chapter 2: Setting Up & Managing Your Google Account

Creating and managing your Google Account is the first step in unlocking the full potential of Google Workspace and its associated services. In this chapter, we will guide you through the process of creating a Google Account, personalizing your profile, managing account settings, and understanding Google's storage plans. Whether you're using a Google account for personal or business purposes, managing your settings effectively is crucial to maintaining security, privacy, and a seamless user experience.

Creating a Google Account

A Google Account serves as your gateway to all of Google's services, including Gmail, Google Drive, Google Calendar, and Google Workspace apps. Here's how to create a Google account:

1. **Visit the Google Account Creation Page**:
   Go to the Google Account sign-up page at
   https://accounts.google.com/signup.

Sign in

Use your Google Account

Email or phone

Forgot email?

Not your computer? Use Guest mode to sign in privately.
Learn more

Create account

For my personal use

For my child

Englis   Help   Privacy   Terms

For work or my business

2. **Enter Your Information**:
   Fill in your first and last name, a preferred username, and password. Your username will become your Gmail email address (e.g., yourname@gmail.com).

Create your Google Account

First name
Elena

Last name
Casarosa

Username
ecasarosa98   @gmail.com

You can use letters, numbers & periods

Use my current email address instead

Password
········

Confirm
········

Use 8 or more characters with a mix of letters, numbers & symbols

☐ Show password

Sign in instead   Next

One account. All of Google
working for you.

English (United States) ▾   Help   Privacy   Terms

3. **Verify Your Phone Number**:
   Google requires a phone number to help secure your account. You'll receive a verification code via SMS to confirm your identity.
4. **Provide Recovery Information**:
   Enter an alternative email address or a security question to help recover your account in case you forget your password.

14

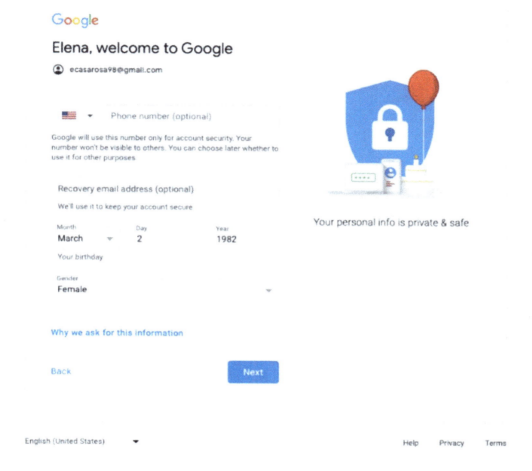

5. **Agree to the Terms**:
   Review Google's Privacy & Terms, then click "I Agree" to proceed.

Google

Privacy and Terms

To create a Google Account, you'll need to agree to the Terms of Service below.

In addition, when you create an account, we process your information as described in our Privacy Policy, including these key points:

Data we process when you use Google

- When you set up a Google Account, we store information you give us like your name, email address, and telephone number.
- When you use Google services to do things like write a message in Gmail or comment on a YouTube video, we store the information you create.
- When you search for a restaurant on Google Maps or watch a video on YouTube, for example, we process information about that activity – including information like the video you watched, device IDs, IP addresses, cookie data, and location.
- We also process the kinds of information described above when you use apps or sites that use Google services like ads, Analytics, and the YouTube video player.

You're in control of the data we collect & how it's used

6. **Set Up Additional Security** (optional but recommended):
   After creating your account, Google will prompt you to set up recovery options and security settings, such as two-factor authentication, to protect your account.

Once your account is created, you're ready to use Google services and explore Google Workspace.

Setting Up Your Profile Picture & Personal Information

Personalizing your Google Account with a profile picture and updated information can help others identify you easily, especially when using services like Gmail or Google Meet.

1. **Adding a Profile Picture**:
   o Go to Google Account and click on **Personal Info**.
   o Under the **Profile** section, you will see the option to add or change your photo.
   o Click on the camera icon and upload a photo from your computer or select one from your Google Photos.
2. **Editing Personal Information**:
   o You can update your name, contact information, and personal bio directly within the **Personal Info** section.
   o Ensure your contact email and phone number are accurate to avoid issues with account recovery or notifications.

A well-set profile picture not only adds a personal touch but also helps with professional branding, especially if you're using Google Workspace for business purposes.

Managing Google Account Settings (Security, Privacy, & Notifications)

Google provides robust tools for managing your account settings, from security and privacy to notifications and personalization. Here's how to manage each:

1. Security Settings

To protect your Google Account and personal information, it's essential to configure your security settings properly:

- **Enable Two-Factor Authentication (2FA)**:
  In the **Security** section of your Google Account settings, turn on **2-Step Verification** to add an extra layer of security. This ensures that even if someone knows your password, they won't be able to access your account without your phone.
- **Review Your Devices & Sign-ins**:
  You can view the devices that have accessed your account under the **Your Devices** section. If you notice any unfamiliar activity, immediately remove the device and change your password.
- **Security Checkup**:
  Google offers a **Security Checkup** tool that walks you through recommended security improvements, such as updating your password or reviewing connected apps.

2. Privacy Settings

Your Google Account contains sensitive data, so ensuring that it's private is important:

- **Manage Activity Controls**:
  Under **Privacy & Personalization**, you can adjust settings related to your search history, YouTube activity, and location history. If you prefer Google not to track certain activities, you can disable the relevant options.

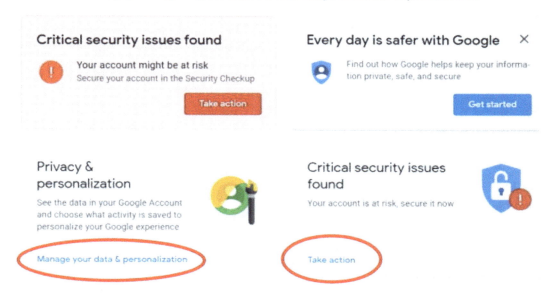

- **Control Who Can See Your Info**:
  Google allows you to manage who can view your profile details. You can set specific visibility options for your name, photo, and other information.

3. Notification Preferences

Google keeps you informed through notifications about your account's activity, app updates, and security alerts:

- **Email & Push Notifications**:
  Under the **Notifications** section, you can opt in or out of various notifications from Google services. Whether it's updates from Google Docs or security alerts, make sure your preferences reflect what you actually need.
- **Personalized Alerts**:
  You can also receive notifications about your account's security, such as suspicious login attempts or password change notifications.

Understanding Google Storage Plans & Upgrading Storage

Google provides cloud storage for free through Google Drive, but if you need more space, you can upgrade to a paid plan. Here's how storage works and how you can manage or upgrade your storage:

1. Google Storage Basics

Every Google Account comes with **15GB of free storage**, shared across Gmail, Google Drive, and Google Photos. As you upload emails, files, and photos, this free space can fill up quickly. You can check how much space you have left by going to the **Storage** section of your Google Account.

2. Upgrading Storage with Google One

If you find yourself running low on storage, you can upgrade your Google storage plan using **Google One**:

- **Google One Plans**:
    - 100GB: $1.99/month
    - 200GB: $2.99/month
    - 2TB: $9.99/month
    - Larger plans are also available for even more storage.
- **Benefits of Google One**:
    - Increased storage for Gmail, Drive, and Photos
    - Additional family sharing (up to 5 people)
    - Access to Google's premium support team
    - Extra features in Google Photos, such as higher-quality backups
    - Google One subscribers also receive occasional perks, such as discounts or Google Play credits.

3. Managing Storage

If you need to manage your storage without upgrading:

- **Delete Unnecessary Files**:
  Go through your Google Drive and Gmail account, deleting old or unnecessary files and emails.
- **Empty the Trash**:
  Don't forget to empty the Trash in Gmail and Google Drive, as deleted items still count against your storage quota until they're permanently removed.

Conclusion

By following these steps to create and manage your Google Account, you can enhance your overall experience with Google services. Whether you are setting up your profile, managing security settings, or upgrading your storage, taking the time to customize and safeguard your account will allow you to get the most out of Google Workspace and other Google tools. Proper management of your account also ensures a more secure, personalized, and efficient experience.

Chapter 3: Enhancing Google Workspace Security & Privacy

Google Workspace offers a suite of powerful tools to help individuals and organizations collaborate and store information securely. However, ensuring that your account and data are protected requires configuring certain security and privacy settings. In this chapter, we will walk you through the essential steps for enhancing your Google Workspace account security and privacy. By enabling features like Two-Factor Authentication (2FA) and adjusting privacy settings, you can ensure that your personal and business information remains safe from unauthorized access.

Enabling Two-Factor Authentication (2FA)

Two-Factor Authentication (2FA) is a simple yet effective method to enhance the security of your Google Account. It adds an extra layer of protection by requiring you to verify your identity through a secondary method, such as a text message or an authenticator app, after entering your password.

Steps to Enable 2FA:

1. **Go to Your Google Account**:
   Navigate to your Google Account, then select the **Security** tab from the menu.

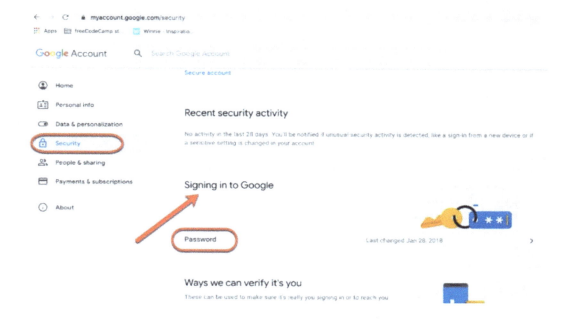

2. **Find Two-Step Verification**:
   Scroll down and select the **2-Step Verification** option. Click on **Get Started**.

Security Checkup

1 issue found

	2-Step Verification Add a backup second step	⌄
	Your devices 2 signed-in devices	⌄
	Recent security events 5 recent events	⌄

3. **Follow the Setup Process**:
    Google will prompt you to enter your password again for verification.
    After that, you can choose the verification method—usually, a phone
    number to receive a text or an authenticator app.

Generated app password

Your app password for your device

your app password

How to use it

Go to the settings for your Google Account in the application or device you are trying to set up. Replace your password with the 16-character password shown above.
Just like your normal password, this app password grants complete access to your Google Account. You won't need to remember it, so don't write it down or share it with anyone.

Email
securesally@gmail.com

Password
••••••••••••

DONE

4. **Confirm Your Settings**:
   Once you've selected your preferred method, Google will guide you through the final steps to ensure everything is working correctly.

By enabling 2FA, even if someone gets hold of your password, they won't be able to access your account without the second verification step.

Managing Google Account Recovery Options

Recovery options are essential for regaining access to your account if you forget your password or get locked out. Google provides several recovery methods, including using a secondary email address and a phone number.

Steps to Manage Recovery Options:

1. **Go to Your Google Account Settings**:
    Visit your Google Account and select **Personal Info** from the menu.
2. **Set Up a Recovery Email & Phone Number**:
    In the **Contact Info** section, add a recovery email address and phone number that will be used if you need to recover your account.

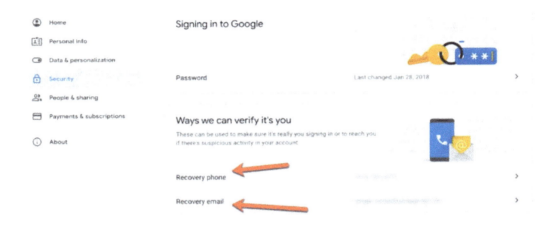

3. **Update Security Questions**:
    While not always necessary, you can also set up a security question for additional account recovery options. This can be useful if you lose access to both your email and phone number.
4. **Test Your Recovery Options**:
    After setting them up, try using your recovery methods to ensure they work.

Having reliable recovery options can help you regain access to your account quickly and easily in case of an emergency.

Adjusting Privacy & Data Sharing Settings

Managing your privacy and the data you share with others is crucial for maintaining control over your personal and professional information. Google allows you to customize your privacy settings and control what information is visible to others.

Steps to Adjust Privacy Settings:

1. **Navigate to Google Account Settings**:
   Open your Google Account and go to the **Privacy & Personalization** section.
2. **Review Activity Controls**:
   You can choose to disable or enable certain activity tracking, such as Web & App Activity, Location History, and YouTube History. If you prefer not to have Google track your actions, disable these options.
3. **Manage Ad Personalization**:
   In the **Ad Settings** section, you can control whether Google uses your data to personalize ads. Turn off ad personalization if you want to stop Google from tracking your preferences for targeted ads.
4. **Data Sharing Options**:
   You can choose which Google services and apps have access to your data. You can also review and delete information from Google's cloud storage as needed.

Taking time to adjust your privacy settings ensures that you only share the information you want to and that your data stays private.

Reviewing & Managing Connected Apps

Connected apps are third-party services that are linked to your Google Account. While these apps can enhance functionality, they also pose security risks if not properly managed. You should regularly review the apps connected to your Google Account and remove any that are no longer necessary.

Steps to Manage Connected Apps:

1. **Go to the Apps Section**:
    In your Google Account settings, select **Security**, then scroll down to the **Third-party apps with account access** section.
2. **Review App Permissions**:
    Look through the list of apps and services that have access to your Google Account. For each app, you'll see the level of access it has to your account.
3. **Remove Unwanted Apps**:
    If you come across any apps you no longer use or trust, select the app and click **Remove Access** to revoke its permission.
4. **Manage App Permissions for New Apps**:
    When adding a new app, always review the permissions it requests before granting access. If an app asks for unnecessary permissions, it's a good idea to reconsider whether you should grant access.

By regularly managing connected apps, you ensure that your Google Account stays secure and that only trusted services have access to your data.

Conclusion

Configuring Google Workspace security and privacy settings is a crucial step in protecting both personal and business information. By enabling Two-Factor Authentication, managing your recovery options, adjusting privacy settings, and reviewing connected apps, you are taking significant steps to enhance your account's security. These proactive measures help ensure that your data is protected, reducing the risk of unauthorized access and maintaining control over the information you share online.

PART 2: Communication & Collaboration Tools

Chapter 4: Mastering Gmail for Optimal Email Efficiency

G mail is one of the most widely used email platforms, offering powerful tools for communication, organization, and productivity. In this chapter, you'll learn how to take full advantage of Gmail's features to improve your email experience. From composing well-organized emails to managing your inbox efficiently, this guide will cover everything you need to know to use Gmail like a pro.

Exploring the Gmail Interface

When you first open Gmail, you are greeted with a clean and user-friendly interface. To navigate it efficiently, you should understand the layout and key features that help you stay organized.

Key Areas of Gmail's Interface:

1. **Inbox & Labels**: Your main inbox shows incoming emails, while labels allow you to categorize emails based on topics or projects.
2. **Search Bar**: Located at the top, it helps you quickly locate any email, contact, or attachment.
3. **Sidebar**: This section gives you easy access to other Gmail tools, such as Google Chat, Google Meet, and Google Tasks.
4. **Compose Button**: Found on the left-hand side, this button allows you to start a new email.

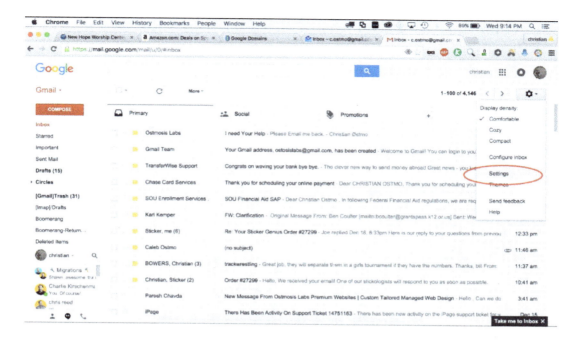

Understanding Gmail's layout will allow you to navigate the platform more quickly and streamline your workflow.

Crafting & Structuring Emails Like a Pro

The way you compose emails plays a significant role in how your message is received. In Gmail, you can easily compose professional-looking emails with proper formatting and structure.

Tips for Composing Emails:

1. **Clear Subject Line**: Always write a concise and descriptive subject to help the recipient understand the purpose of your email.
2. **Professional Greeting**: Start with a polite greeting to set a positive tone, such as "Dear [Name]" or "Hello [Name]."
3. **Proper Email Body**: Use short paragraphs and bullet points to break up long sections of text. This makes it easier to read.

4. **Polite Closing**: Sign off with a friendly closing, such as "Best regards" or "Sincerely," followed by your name.
5. **Formatting Options**: Gmail provides rich text options like bold, italics, and underline to highlight important points.

By following these steps, your emails will be clear, well-organized, and more likely to get the desired response.

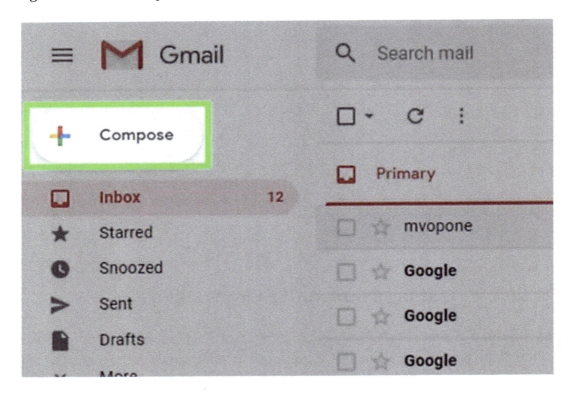

Using Labels, Filters & Stars to Organize Your Emails

With the increasing volume of emails, organizing them is crucial to maintaining an efficient inbox. Gmail provides several features to help you sort and prioritize your emails.

Ways to Organize Your Emails:

1. **Labels**: Think of labels as digital folders. You can create and assign labels to emails to categorize them by project, client, or urgency.

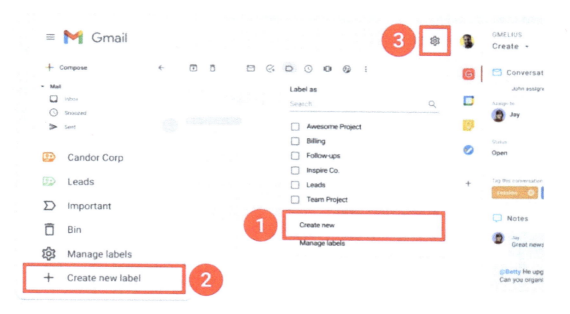

2. **Filters**: Filters help you automatically sort incoming emails based on criteria like sender, subject, or keywords. For example, you can create a filter to send all emails from a specific client directly to a designated folder.

3. **Stars**: Use stars to mark important emails that you need to revisit later. You can customize the stars to assign different colors or symbols.

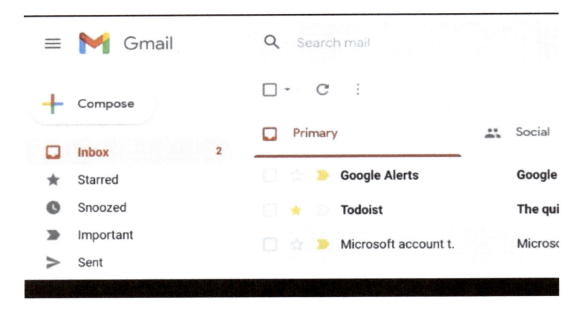

By organizing your inbox with labels, filters, and stars, you'll be able to easily find and manage emails, improving both productivity and organization.

Setting Up Auto-Responses & Email Signatures

Auto-replies and email signatures are great for saving time and ensuring consistency in your communication. Whether you're out of the office or just need a professional sign-off, Gmail allows you to automate certain email functions.

How to Set Up Auto-Responses:

1. **Out of Office Reply**: In Gmail's settings, you can set up an out-of-office reply that automatically informs people when you're unavailable. This is useful for vacations or extended breaks.
2. **Custom Responses**: You can create custom templates for frequently asked questions or common responses, saving time when replying to similar inquiries.

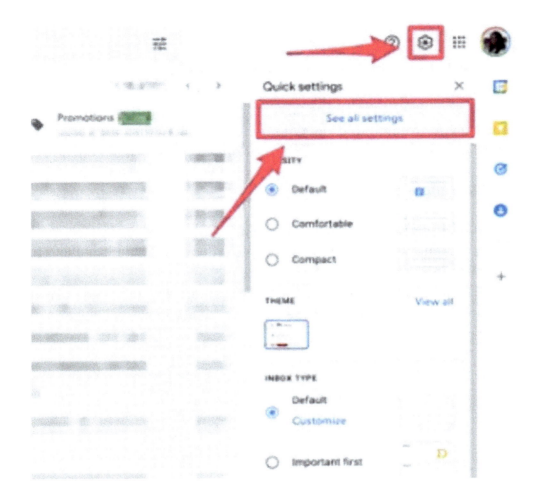

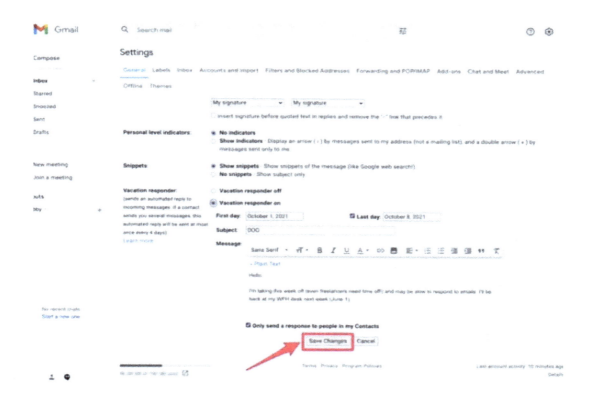

Email Signatures:

Set up an email signature that is automatically included at the end of your emails. This can contain your contact information, job title, or any other relevant details you'd like recipients to see.

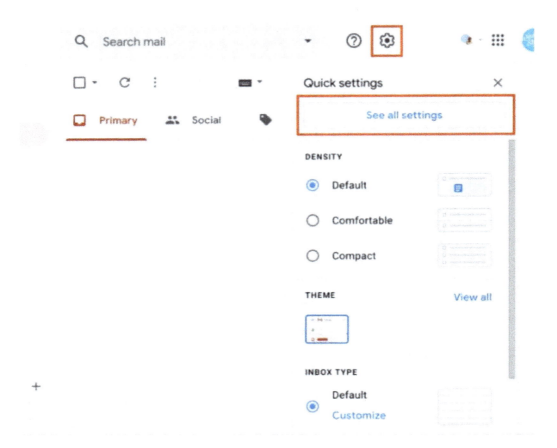

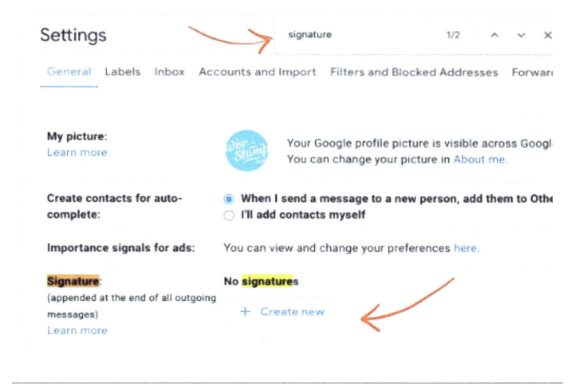

Boosting Efficiency with Gmail Shortcuts

Gmail shortcuts are a great way to save time by eliminating the need to navigate menus and buttons. Using keyboard shortcuts will help you navigate your inbox and perform tasks much faster.

Most Useful Gmail Shortcuts:

1. **C**: Compose a new email.
2. **E**: Archive the selected email.
3. **/ (Slash)**: Quickly jump to the search bar.
4. **Shift + U**: Mark email as unread.
5. **Shift + N**: Go to the next email in the thread.

You can view and customize Gmail shortcuts by going to the **Settings** gear icon, then choosing **See all settings > General > Keyboard shortcuts**.

Shortcut	Function
C	Compose new email
R	Reply to an email
F	Forward an email
Ctrl + Enter	Send email
E	Archive email
Shift + U	Mark as unread

Scheduling Emails for Later Delivery

Sometimes, you may want to compose an email but send it at a more appropriate time. Gmail lets you schedule emails for future delivery, ensuring your message reaches the recipient when they're most likely to see it.

Steps to Schedule an Email:

1. Compose your email as usual.
2. Instead of clicking **Send**, click the **down arrow** next to it and select **Schedule send**.

example@mail.com

How to Schedule an Email in Gmail on Desktop

Hi John,
Hope this meets you well. This is a step-by-step guide on how to schedule an email in Gmail on your desktop computer

How to Schedule an Email in Gmail on Desktop   _ ⤢ ✕

example@mail.com

How to Schedule an Email in Gmail on Desktop

Hi John,
Hope this meets you well. This is a step-by-step guide on how to schedule an email in Gmail on your desktop computer

3. Choose the desired time and date for the email to be sent.

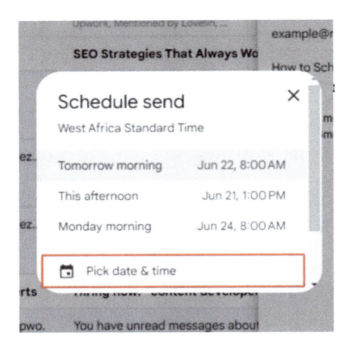

4. Gmail will send the email at the time you've specified.

This feature is useful for sending reminders, time-sensitive information, or follow-up emails at the right moment.

Managing Spam & Unwanted Emails

Spam emails can quickly fill up your inbox and reduce your productivity. Fortunately, Gmail provides effective tools to help you manage and minimize spam.

Ways to Handle Spam:

1. **Mark as Spam**: If an email looks suspicious or unwanted, click the **Report Spam** button to automatically send it to the spam folder.
2. **Unsubscribe**: Gmail often detects subscription emails and provides an **Unsubscribe** button at the top of the message to stop receiving future emails from that sender.
3. **Create Filters for Spam**: If you regularly receive similar spam emails, you can create filters to automatically send these emails to the trash or a specific folder.

By using Gmail's spam management tools, you can keep your inbox clutter-free and focus on the emails that matter most.

Conclusion

Mastering Gmail's features is key to making your email experience more efficient and productive. From composing professional emails and organizing your inbox to scheduling messages and managing spam, Gmail provides a robust set of tools to help you stay on top of your communication. By learning how to use these features, you'll be able to manage your emails like a pro, saving time and keeping your inbox organized.

Chapter 5: Streamlining Team Communication with Google Chat

G oogle Chat is an essential tool for instant messaging and team collaboration within Google Workspace. It allows individuals and teams to communicate quickly, share files, and collaborate on projects seamlessly. This chapter will guide you through the key features of Google Chat and show you how to make the most of this powerful tool for better team productivity.

Exploring the Google Chat Interface

Google Chat's interface is designed to be simple, intuitive, and easy to navigate. The interface allows you to stay connected with your team and organize conversations efficiently.

Key Areas of Google Chat's Interface:

1. **Left Sidebar**: This area shows your active conversations, direct messages (DMs), and spaces.
2. **Conversations Window**: Here, you can view messages exchanged with your team members or groups.
3. **Search Bar**: Located at the top, the search bar enables you to quickly find conversations, messages, or files.
4. **User Profile & Settings**: This area allows you to manage your account settings, notification preferences, and status.

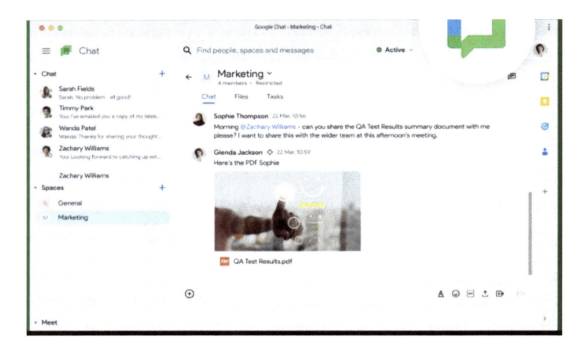

By familiarizing yourself with these sections, you'll be able to navigate Google Chat efficiently and stay on top of important messages.

Creating & Managing Conversations

One of the primary functions of Google Chat is initiating and managing conversations. Whether you're communicating with a single person or a team, setting up and managing conversations is easy.

How to Start a New Conversation:

1. Click the **+ (Plus)** icon or **New Chat** option.

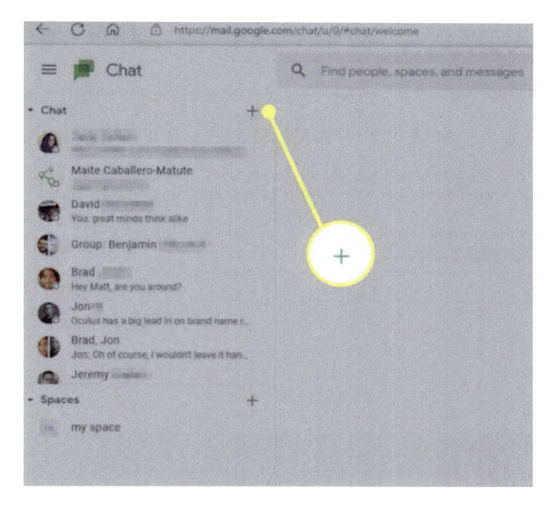

2. Enter the names or email addresses of the people you wish to communicate with.
3. Select **Create** or **Send** to start the conversation.

Managing Existing Conversations:

1. **Mute Conversations**: If you want to stop receiving notifications for a conversation, click on the chat, go to settings, and select **Mute**.
2. **Pin Important Chats**: Pin important conversations to the top for easy access.
3. **Mark as Unread**: If you want to revisit a conversation later, you can mark it as unread, ensuring you don't forget about it.

Google Chat makes it easy to manage all your communications, ensuring important messages don't get lost.

Collaborating with Group Chats & Spaces

Google Chat also supports group messaging and collaborative spaces, ideal for project-based discussions, team coordination, or socializing with colleagues.

Creating a Space:

1. Click the **+** icon next to the Spaces section.

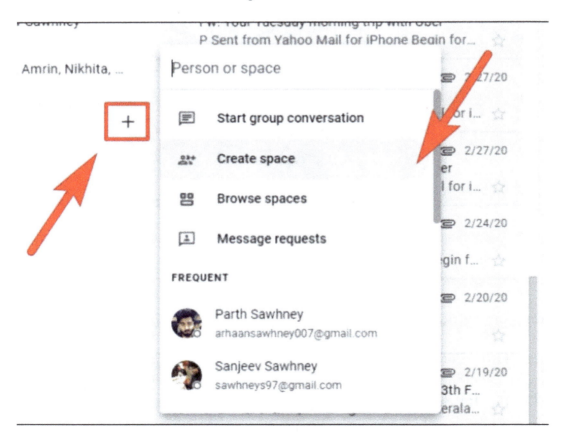

2. Choose whether the space will be **General** or **Restricted** (for specific team members).

3. Add participants and give the space a name.

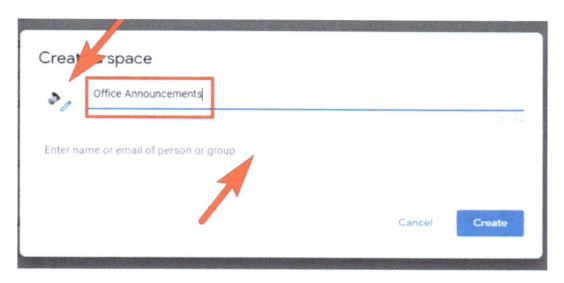

4. Once created, you can share files, have threaded conversations, and even use it for collaborative brainstorming.

Spaces allow teams to work together on projects, share feedback, and hold discussions all in one place, improving workflow and efficiency.

Sending Files, Links & Attachments

Sharing files and links is essential for efficient collaboration. Google Chat enables you to send documents, images, videos, and links directly within your conversations.

How to Share Files & Links:

1. **Send Files**: Click the **paperclip icon** (or drag and drop) to attach a file from Google Drive or your device.
2. **Share Links**: Simply copy and paste any URL, and it will automatically be formatted as a clickable link.

3. **Send Google Docs/Sheets/Slides**: You can also directly share Google Docs, Sheets, and Slides by clicking on the **Google Drive icon** and selecting the document you wish to share.

This feature enhances communication by making it easy to send the right information at the right time.

Integrating Google Chat with Gmail

Google Chat integrates seamlessly with Gmail, making it easier to communicate without needing to switch between apps.

How to Use Google Chat in Gmail:

1. Open Gmail and click on the **Chat** icon on the left-hand sidebar.
2. You can start a direct message or join an existing space directly from Gmail.
3. If you receive a message in Google Chat while working in Gmail, you can reply to it without leaving your inbox.

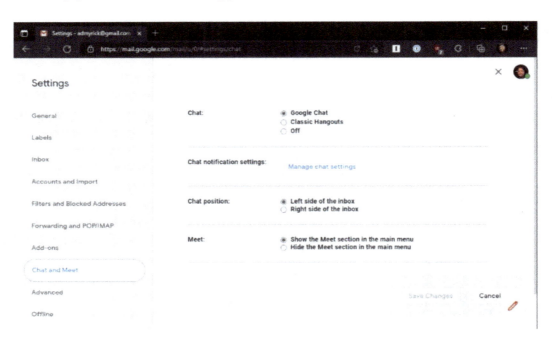

By connecting Gmail and Google Chat, you streamline your workflow and reduce the need to jump between multiple tabs.

Conclusion

Google Chat is an invaluable tool for team communication and collaboration. By understanding its interface, creating and managing conversations, utilizing group chats and spaces, sharing files and links, and integrating it with Gmail, you'll be well on your way to improving your team's productivity and communication.

Chapter 6: Hosting Seamless Video Meetings with Google Meet

Google Meet is a powerful tool for hosting video calls and virtual meetings. Whether you're conducting one-on-one meetings, team conferences, or large webinars, Google Meet provides everything you need for smooth and productive online collaboration. In this chapter, we'll walk through the steps to set up, manage, and maximize your Google Meet video calls.

Setting Up a Google Meet Video Call

Setting up a video call with Google Meet is quick and easy. Whether you're scheduling ahead or starting an impromptu meeting, this process will get you ready to connect with your team instantly.

Steps to Set Up a Google Meet Call:

1. **Option 1: From Google Calendar**
   - Open Google Calendar and create a new event.
   - Click on **Add Google Meet video conferencing**.
   - Invite participants by adding their email addresses in the "Guests" section.
   - Save the event and share the invite link with attendees.
2. **Option 2: Instant Call**
   - Open Google Meet.
   - Click on **New Meeting** and select **Create a meeting for later**, or **Start an instant meeting**, or **Schedule in Google Calendar**.

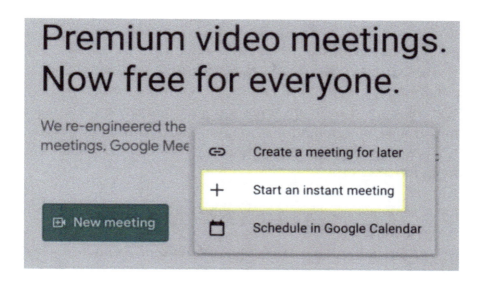

- Copy the meeting link or send invites directly.

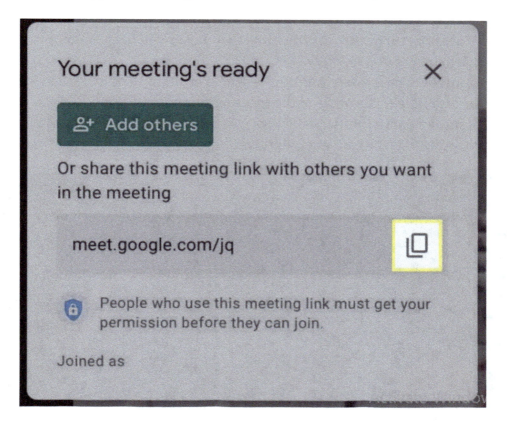

Once set up, you can start the meeting by simply clicking the link.

Inviting Participants & Managing Permissions

Google Meet allows you to invite others to join the meeting and manage their permissions to ensure a smooth meeting experience.

How to Invite Participants:

1. During the meeting setup, simply enter the participants' email addresses to send invitations.
2. If you've already created a meeting, you can send an invite via the meeting link or directly from the Google Meet interface.

Managing Permissions:

1. **Mute Participants**: As the meeting host, you can mute or unmute participants as necessary.
2. **Control Screen Sharing**: Decide who can share their screen by enabling or disabling this feature in the meeting settings.
3. **Remove Participants**: If needed, you can remove any participant from the meeting to ensure no interruptions.

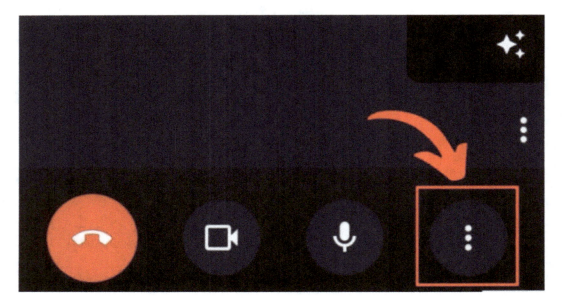

By managing these settings, you'll maintain control over the flow of the meeting and ensure it runs smoothly.

Enhancing Your Meeting with Background Effects & Filters

Personalizing your Google Meet video feed can add a bit of fun or professionalism to your meeting. Use background effects or filters to change your environment or enhance your appearance.

Using Background Effects:

1. Click on the **three dots** (More options) in the lower-right corner.

2. Select **Change background** to blur your background, use a predefined virtual background, or upload your own.

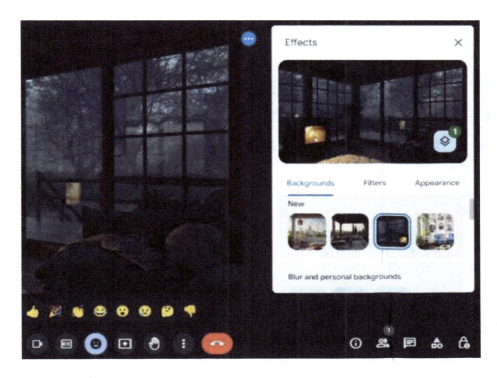

This is especially useful if you're in a space that's not ideal for meetings or if you want to maintain a level of privacy.

Applying Filters:

Google Meet also offers a range of filters to improve your appearance during video calls. Adjust the filter to suit your preference and ensure you look your best on camera.

Sharing Your Screen & Presenting Slides

Screen sharing and presenting content is a key feature of Google Meet, especially for team collaborations, virtual presentations, or brainstorming sessions.

How to Share Your Screen:

1. Click on the **Present Now** button at the bottom-right corner.
2. Choose between **Your entire screen**, **A window**, or **A tab** to share the desired content.

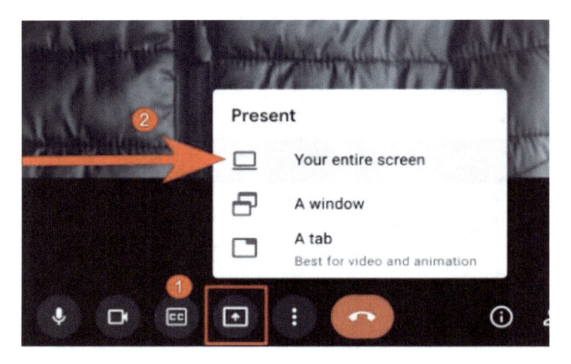

You can present slides, documents, or any other type of content. Be sure to select the correct window or screen to ensure a smooth presentation.

Presenting Slides:

When presenting slides, consider having your slides open in Google Slides or another application before the meeting starts. This allows you to present seamlessly and keep your focus on the content rather than switching between tabs.

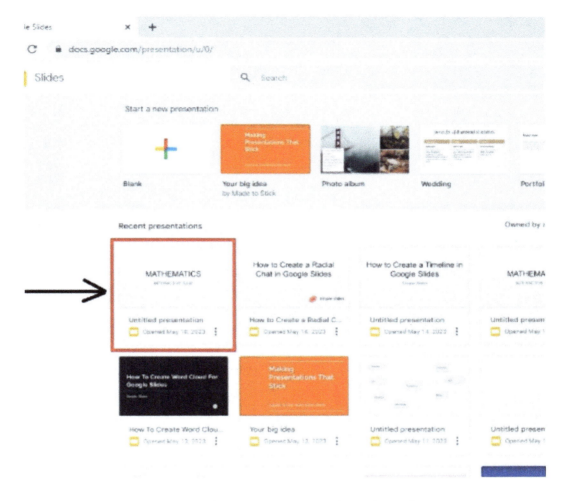

In Google Slides, Click slideshow drop-down button.

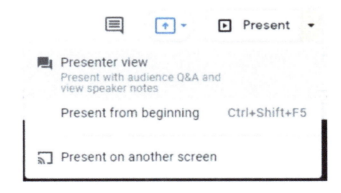

*Use the **presenter view** in Google slide*

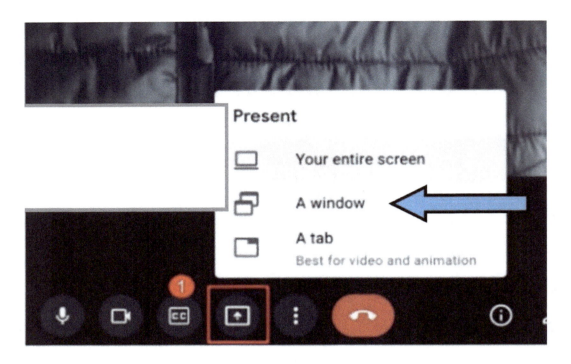

*Go back to Google Meet and go to **Present now> A Window***

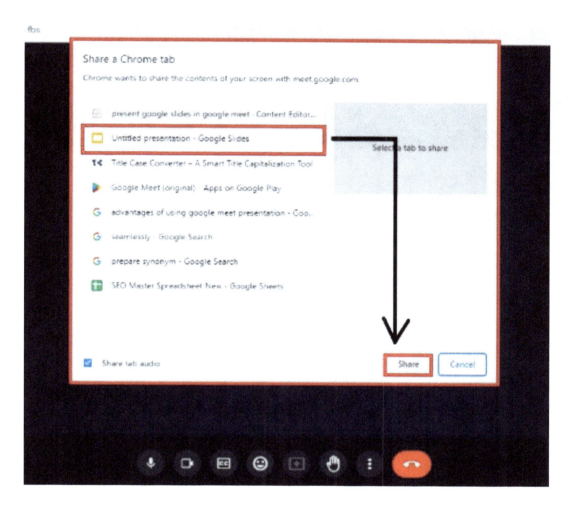

*Now select the Google Slides window and click **Share***

MATHEMATICS

INTERACTIVE QUIZ

Recording & Saving Meetings

Recording meetings is essential for future reference, especially if there are important discussions, decisions, or information shared during the session. Google Meet offers an easy way to record and save your meetings for later review.

How to Record a Google Meet Meeting:

1. As the host, click on the **three dots** in the lower-right corner.
2. Select **Record meeting**.

3. Once the meeting is over, the recording will automatically be saved to the meeting organizer's Google Drive, in the "Meet Recordings" folder.

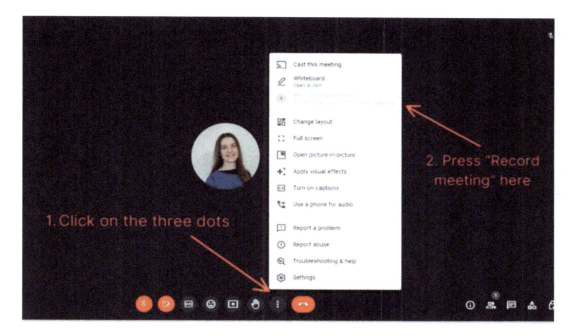

This is perfect for those who want to review the meeting later or share it with others who couldn't attend.

Conclusion

Google Meet is a comprehensive and efficient platform for hosting and managing virtual meetings. From setting up a video call to inviting participants, using background effects, sharing screens, and recording meetings, this tool provides all the features needed to facilitate smooth and productive online meetings.

PART 3: Productivity & File Management

Chapter 7: Mastering Google Drive for Storage, Organization & Collaboration

G oogle Drive is a cloud-based storage service that enables users to store, manage, and share files effortlessly. Whether you're an individual looking to keep documents organized or a business collaborating on projects, Google Drive offers a seamless solution for file management. This chapter explores the essential features of Google Drive, from uploading and organizing files to sharing and restoring previous file versions.

Uploading & Downloading Files in Google Drive

Google Drive supports various file formats, making it easy to store documents, images, videos, and more. Uploading and downloading files is straightforward and can be done through the web, desktop, or mobile app.

Uploading Files & Folders

1. **Via Web Browser:**
   - Open Google Drive.
   - Click on **+ New** in the top-left corner.

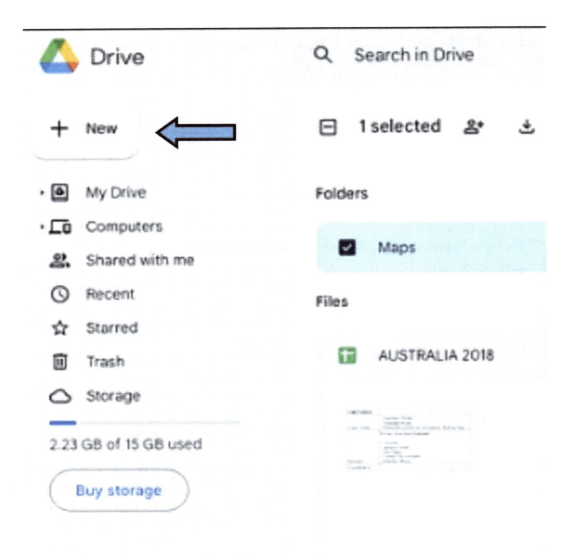

o   Select **File upload** or **Folder upload** and choose the files/folders from your computer.

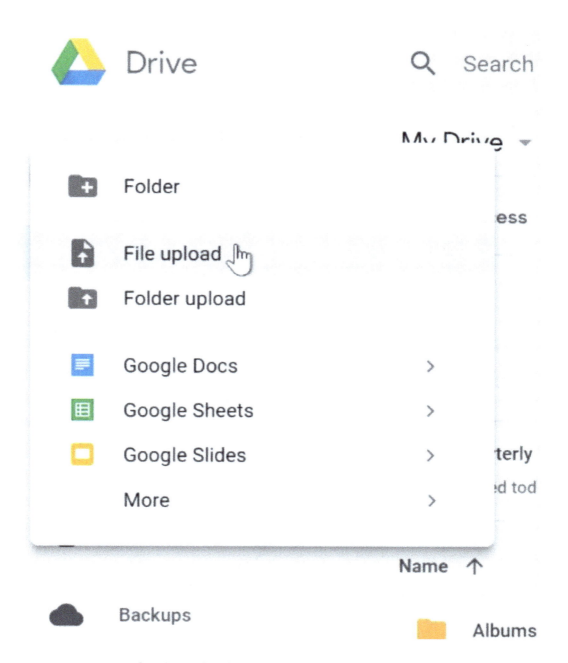

- Wait for the upload to complete; the files will appear in your Drive.
2. **Via Drag & Drop:**
  - Simply drag a file from your computer and drop it into Google Drive.

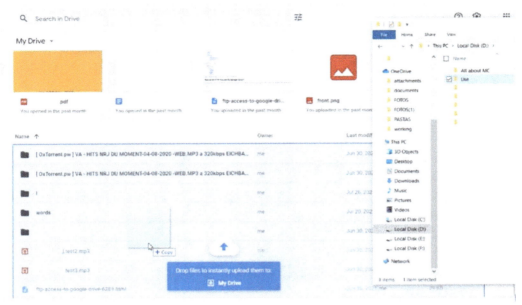

Drag and Drop Files from PC to Google Drive

3. **Using the Google Drive Desktop App:**
   - Install the **Google Drive for Desktop** application.
   - Drag files into your synced Google Drive folder, and they will automatically upload.

Downloading Files & Folders

- Right-click any file in Google Drive and select **Download** to save it to your computer.
- To download multiple files, hold **Ctrl (Windows) / Command (Mac)** and select the files before clicking **Download**.
- Entire folders can be downloaded as ZIP files.

Creating & Organizing Folders

Keeping your Google Drive tidy is essential for quick access to files. Proper folder management makes navigation easier and improves productivity.

How to Create Folders in Google Drive:

1. Click on **+ New** and select **Folder**.

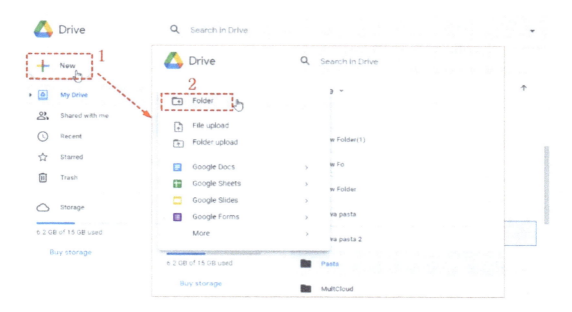

2. Give your folder a meaningful name and click **Create**.

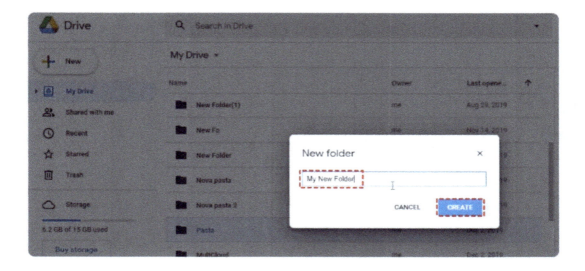

3. Drag and drop files into the folder for better organization.

Best Practices for Organizing Your Drive:

Use a Clear Folder Structure – Create separate folders for work, personal projects, and other categories.
Color Code Folders – Right-click a folder, select **Change color**, and assign colors to easily distinguish between them.
Star Important Files – Mark essential files as starred for quick access under the **Starred** section.

Sharing Files with Different Access Levels

Google Drive allows file sharing with varying levels of control. You can grant view-only, comment, or edit access depending on your needs.

How to Share a File or Folder:

1. Right-click on a file/folder and select **Share**.

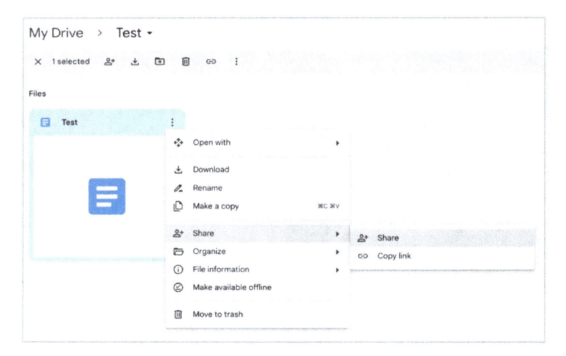

2. Enter the email addresses of the people you want to share it with.
3. Choose the appropriate permission level:
   o **Viewer** – Can see the file but cannot edit or comment.
   o **Commenter** – Can leave comments but cannot make direct changes.
   o **Editor** – Can make changes to the document.
4. Click **Send** to notify recipients.

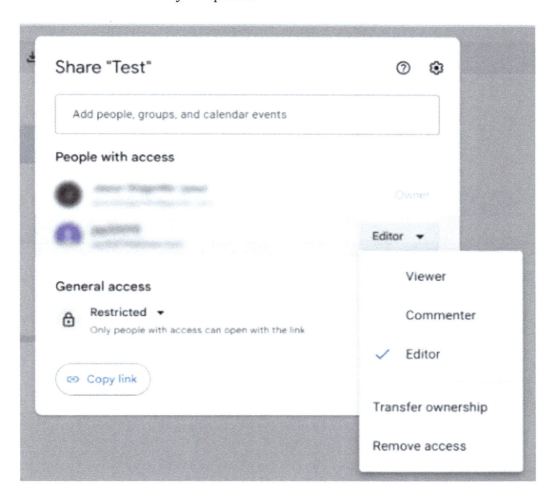

Generating a Shareable Link:

1. Click **Get link** in the share window.

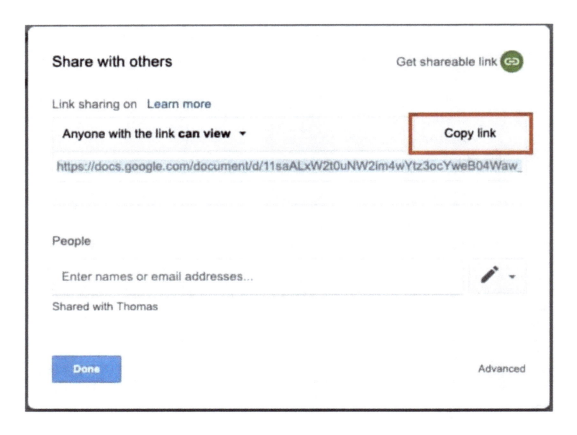

2. Adjust access settings:
    o **Restricted** – Only specified users can access.
    o **Anyone with the link** – Anyone with the link can access (you can still set view, comment, or edit permissions).
3. Copy and share the link as needed.

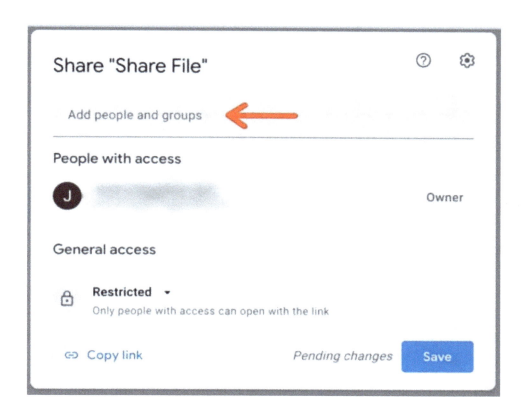

Collaborating on Shared Files

Google Drive integrates seamlessly with Google Docs, Sheets, and Slides, allowing multiple users to collaborate on a document in real-time.

Key Collaboration Features:

- **Live Editing** – See changes as they happen, with each user's cursor marked in a different color.
- **Commenting & Suggestions** – Leave feedback by highlighting text and clicking the **Comment** button.
- **Version History** – View and restore previous versions of the document by clicking **File > Version history**.
- **Activity Dashboard** – Track who viewed and edited the document for better team coordination.

Managing File Versions & Restoring Older Versions

Accidentally made changes to a document? Google Drive keeps track of previous versions, allowing you to revert when needed.

How to View & Restore Previous Versions:

1. Right-click a file and select **Version history > See version history**.
2. A panel will open, displaying all saved versions with timestamps.
3. Click on an earlier version to preview changes.
4. To restore, click **Restore this version**.

For non-Google files (such as PDFs or Word documents), Google Drive retains older versions when re-uploaded with the same name.

Google Drive Keyboard Shortcuts

Boost your efficiency with these useful Google Drive shortcuts:

Shortcut	Action
Shift + T	Create a new Google Docs file
Shift + P	Create a new Google Slides file
Shift + S	Create a new Google Sheets file
/ (forward slash)	Search within Google Drive
N	Rename selected file
Z	Move file to another folder
Shift + A	Select all files
Shift + I	Share selected file
Shift + R	View file revision history

\

Chapter 8: Google Docs – Mastering Document Creation & Collaboration

Google Docs is a powerful, cloud-based word processor that allows users to create, edit, and collaborate on documents in real time. Whether you're writing reports, drafting proposals, or taking notes, Google Docs provides a seamless and feature-rich experience. This chapter explores its interface, formatting tools, collaboration features, and productivity-enhancing functions.

Navigating the Google Docs Interface

When you open Google Docs, the interface is designed for simplicity and efficiency.

Key Sections of Google Docs:

1. **Menu Bar** – Located at the top, this contains all essential tools, including File, Edit, Insert, and Format options.
2. **Toolbar** – Directly below the menu, this provides quick-access icons for text formatting, alignment, inserting elements, and more.
3. **Document Area** – The main workspace where you type and edit content.
4. **Comments & Suggestions Panel** – Used for collaborative editing and feedback.
5. **Explore Tool** – Found in the bottom-right corner, this allows for in-document research and inserting citations.

Formatting Text, Paragraphs, & Styles

Well-structured documents enhance readability and professionalism. Google Docs provides robust formatting tools to customize text and layout.

Text Formatting Options:

- **Bold (Ctrl + B / Cmd + B)** – Emphasize important text.
- **Italic (Ctrl + I / Cmd + I)** – Add emphasis to words or phrases.
- **Underline (Ctrl + U / Cmd + U)** – Highlight key points.

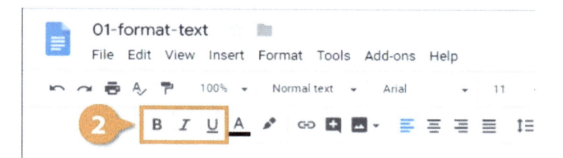

- **Strikethrough (Alt + Shift + 5)** – Indicate deleted or outdated text.

- **Text Color & Highlighting** – Modify the text appearance to improve readability.

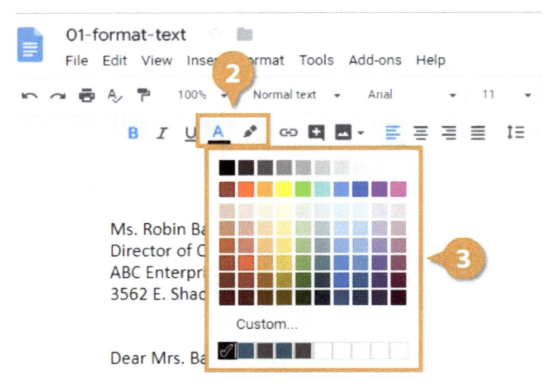

Paragraph Formatting:

- **Alignment (Ctrl + Shift + L/C/R/J)** – Set text to left, center, right, or justified alignment.
- **Line Spacing** – Adjust spacing between lines for better readability.
- **Indentation & Bullet Lists** – Structure information using bullets, numbering, or indentation.

Using Predefined Styles:

Instead of manually formatting text, apply styles from the **Styles Dropdown** (Normal Text, Heading 1, Heading 2, etc.) to maintain consistency.

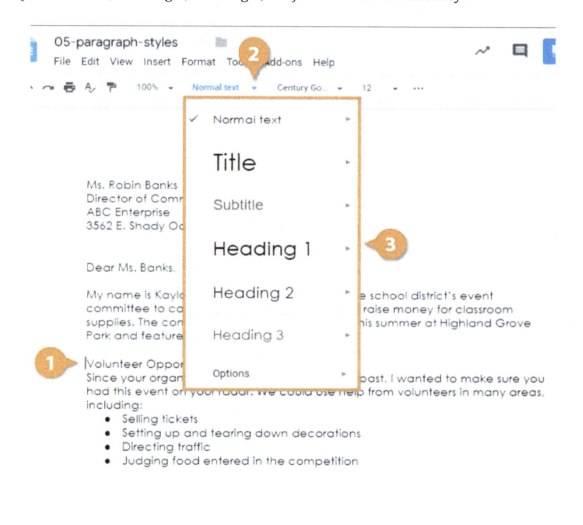

Inserting Images, Tables, Links & Footnotes

Enhance your document by incorporating multimedia and structural elements.

Adding Images:

- Click **Insert > Image** to upload from your device, Google Drive, or the web.

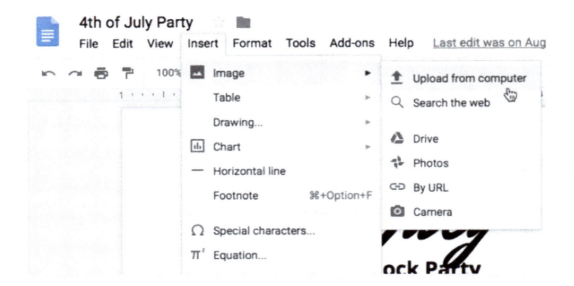

- Resize and reposition images using the image toolbar.

Creating Tables:

- Navigate to **Insert > Table** and select the desired number of rows and columns.

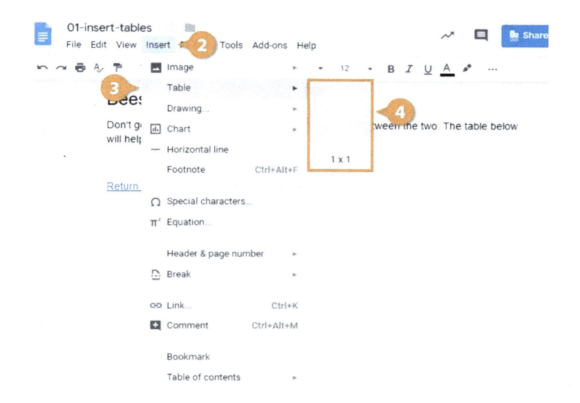

- Use the **Table Properties** option to adjust cell size, borders, and background colors.

Adding Links:

- Highlight text, press **Ctrl + K**, and enter a URL to hyperlink text.
- You can also link to other Google Docs, Sheets, or Slides.

Using Footnotes for Citations:

- Place the cursor where you want a footnote and click **Insert > Footnote**.
- This is useful for academic references or additional explanations.

Collaborating with Others Using Comments & Suggestions

One of Google Docs' most powerful features is real-time collaboration. Multiple users can edit a document simultaneously while tracking changes and leaving feedback.

How to Share a Document:

1. Click **Share** in the top-right corner.
2. Enter email addresses or generate a shareable link.
3. Assign permissions: **Viewer (read-only), Commenter, or Editor.**

Using Comments for Feedback:

- Highlight text and click **Comment** (or use Ctrl + Alt + M).
- Type suggestions or questions, and tag collaborators using **@mentions**.

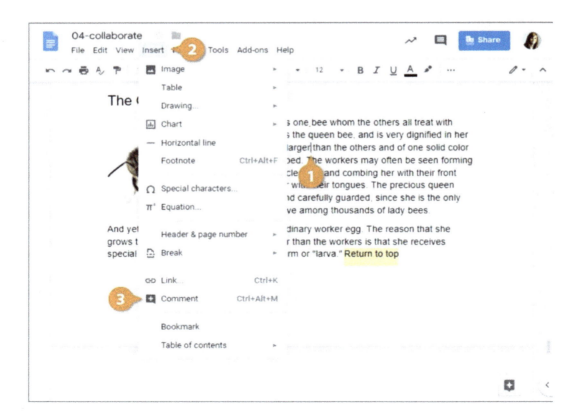

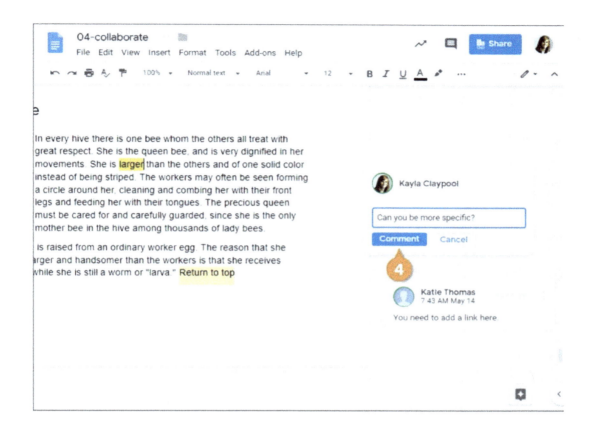

Suggesting Mode for Edits:

Instead of making direct changes, enable **Suggesting Mode** (Ctrl + Shift + Alt + X), which highlights modifications for approval.

And yet the queen bee is raised from an ordinary worker egg. The reason that she grows to be so much larger and handsomer than the workers is that she receives special food and care while she is still a worm or "larva." Return to top

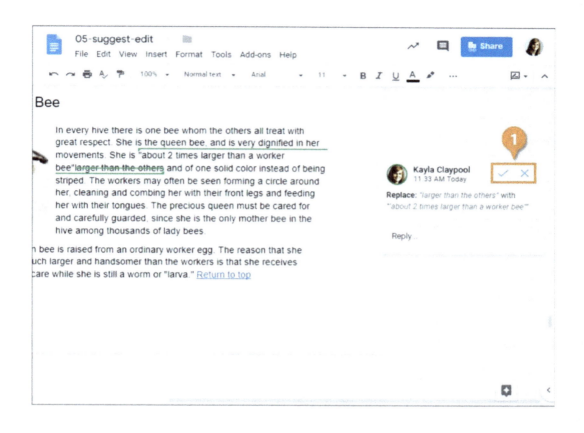

Using Voice Typing & Add-ons for Enhanced Productivity

Voice Typing:

Dictate text instead of typing by enabling **Tools > Voice Typing**. This feature is useful for hands-free note-taking or accessibility purposes.

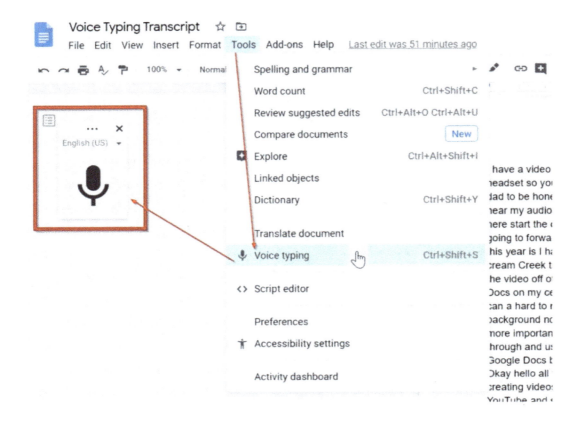

Google Docs Add-ons:

Enhance functionality with add-ons by going to **Extensions > Add-ons > Get add-ons**. Some useful ones include:

- **Grammarly** – Advanced grammar and spell-checking.
- **DocuSign** – E-signatures for documents.
- **Table of Contents** – Automatically generates a structured table of contents.

Format   Tools   **Extensions**   Help

0% ▼   Norn   ☰+ Add-ons

         🖊 Apps Script

         ☰+ Caption Maker

         ☰+ Sorted Paragraphs

Chapter 9: Google Sheets – Unlocking the Power of Spreadsheets

G oogle Sheets is a dynamic cloud-based spreadsheet tool that enables users to organize, analyze, and visualize data. Whether managing budgets, tracking progress, or performing complex calculations, Google Sheets provides powerful features for both beginners and advanced users.

Navigating the Google Sheets Interface

Upon opening Google Sheets, you'll see an interface designed for efficiency and data management.

Key Sections of Google Sheets:

- **Toolbar & Menu Bar** – Provides quick access to essential features like formatting, formulas, and charts.
- **Rows & Columns** – The spreadsheet grid is made up of **rows (numbered 1,2,3...)** and **columns (labeled A, B, C...)**.
- **Formula Bar** – Displays the contents of the selected cell and allows you to enter formulas.
- **Sheet Tabs** – Located at the bottom, these allow you to manage multiple sheets within one file.

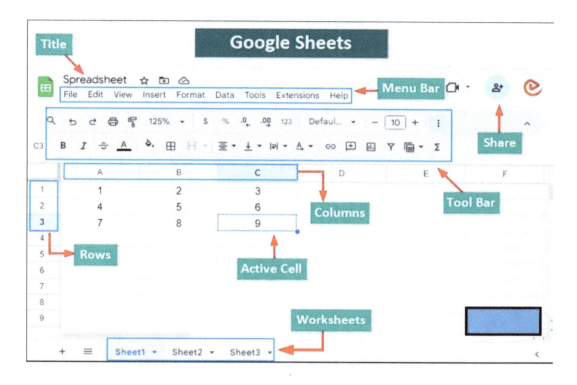

💡 **Tip:** Use Ctrl + / to see a list of all keyboard shortcuts in Google Sheets.

Basic Spreadsheet Formatting

Proper formatting enhances readability and ensures data is presented clearly.

Essential Formatting Options:

- **Bold, Italics, and Colors** – Customize text for better visibility.

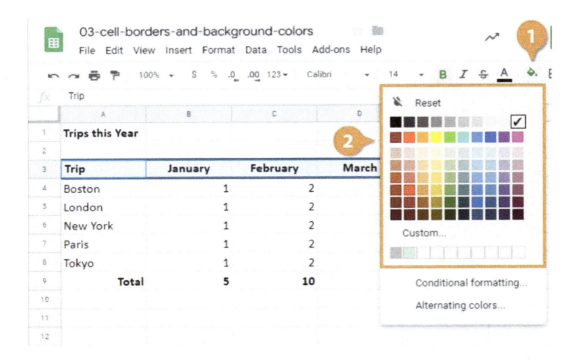

- **Cell Merging** – Combine multiple cells for headers (Format > Merge Cells).
- **Conditional Formatting** – Highlight cells based on rules (Format > Conditional Formatting).
- **Data Validation** – Restrict input types (Data > Data Validation).

💡 **Tip:** Use **freeze panes** (View > Freeze > 1 row) to keep headers visible when scrolling.

Using Formulas & Functions

Google Sheets comes with a vast array of built-in formulas to automate calculations.

Commonly Used Functions:

- **SUM()** – Adds values in a range (=SUM(E2:E4)).

E5 · *fx* =SUM(E2:E4)

	A	B	C	D	E
1	Trainers	Pokeball	Great Balls	Ultra Balls	
2	Iva	2	3	1	6
3	Liam	5	5	2	12
4	Adora	10	2	3	15
5				33 ×	=SUM(E2:E4)

E6 · *fx*

	A	B	C	D	E
1	Trainers	Pokeball	Great Balls	Ultra Balls	
2	Iva	2	3	1	6
3	Liam	5	5	2	12
4	Adora	10	2	3	15
5					33
6					
7					

- **AVERAGE()** – Finds the mean of selected values (=AVERAGE(B1:B10)).
- **VLOOKUP()** – Searches for a value in a table (=VLOOKUP(lookup_value, table_range, column_index, FALSE)).
- **IF()** – Performs logical tests (=IF(A1>10, "High", "Low")).
- **COUNTIF()** – Counts values based on conditions (=COUNTIF(A1:A10, ">50")).

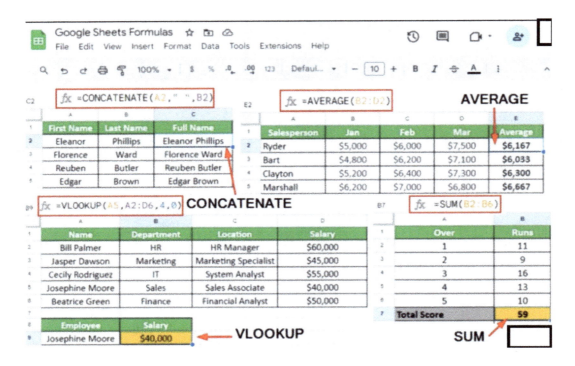

💡 **Tip:** Start typing = in a cell to see a list of suggested functions.

Creating Charts & Graphs for Data Visualization

Visualizing data through charts and graphs helps in analysis and presentations.

Steps to Create a Chart:

1. Select your dataset.
2. Click **Insert > Chart**.

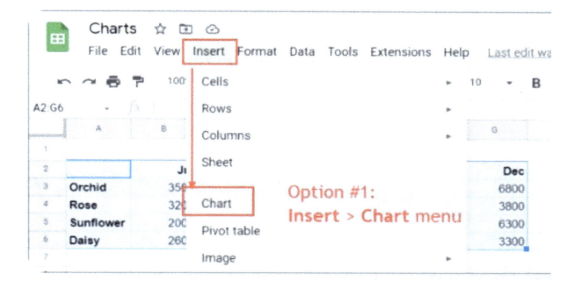

3. Choose the chart type (bar, pie, line, etc.).

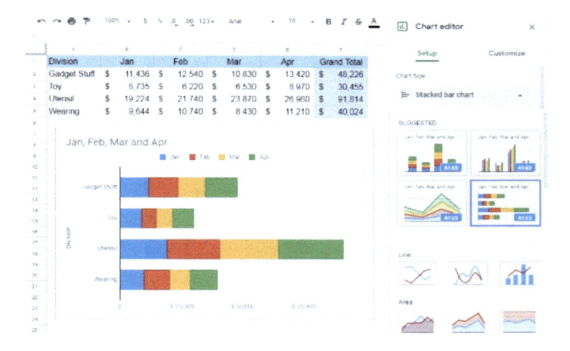

4. Customize labels, colors, and axes using the **Chart Editor**.

💡 **Tip:** Use the **Trendline** option in line charts to forecast data trends.

Collaborating in Google Sheets

Google Sheets allows multiple users to work on the same file in real time.

Collaboration Features:

- **Sharing Permissions** – Click **Share** and set access levels (**Viewer, Commenter, Editor**).

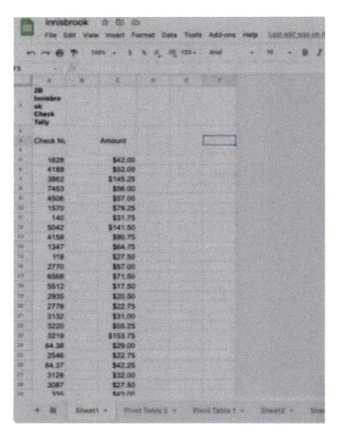

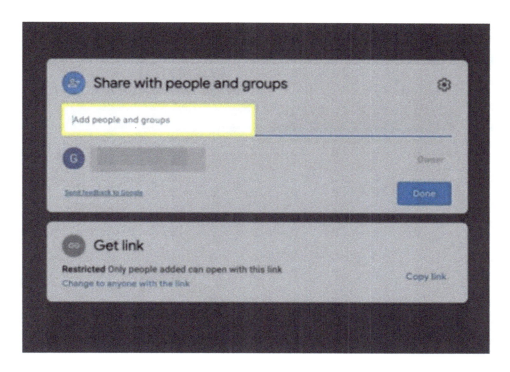

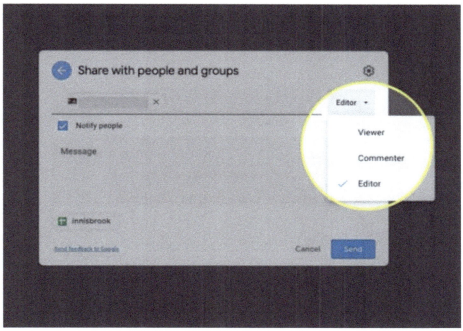

- **Comments & Suggestions** – Highlight a cell and click **Add Comment** for team discussions.

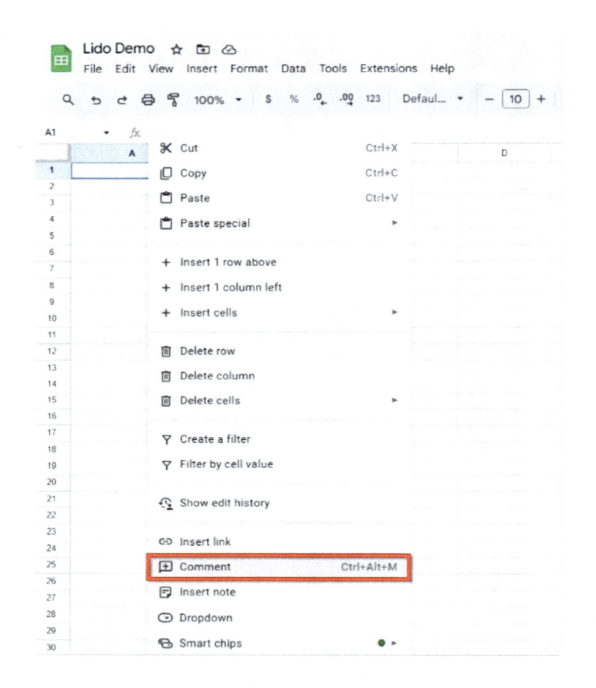

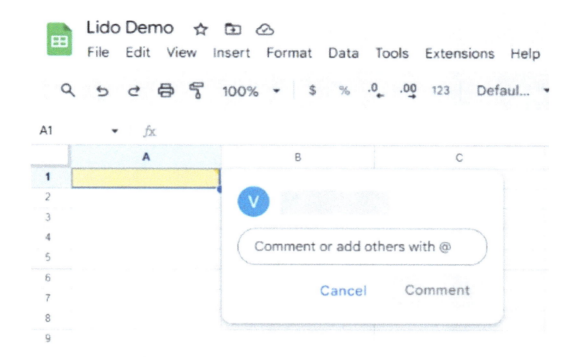

- **Version History** – Restore previous versions via File > Version History.

💡 **Tip:** Use @ to mention collaborators in comments for direct notifications.

Automating Tasks with Google Sheets Macros

Google Sheets allows users to automate repetitive tasks using **Macros**.

How to Create a Macro:

1. Go to **Extensions > Macros > Record Macro**.

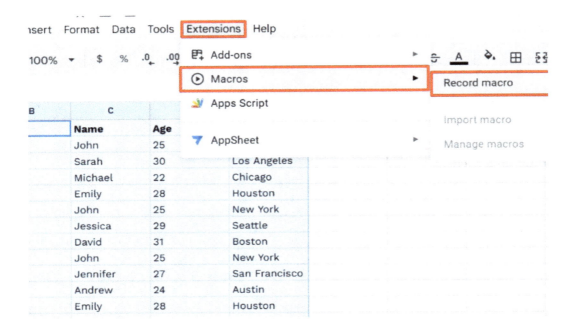

2. Perform the actions you want to automate.
3. Click **Save** and assign a shortcut key.
4. Run the macro anytime to repeat the actions automatically.

💡 **Tip:** Use **Google Apps Script** for advanced automation beyond simple macros.

Conclusion

Google Sheets is a powerful tool for organizing, analyzing, and visualizing data. Mastering its functions, formulas, and collaboration features can significantly improve productivity.

Chapter 10: Google Slides – Crafting Engaging Presentations

Google Slides is a versatile, cloud-based presentation tool that enables users to create, design, and deliver visually appealing slideshows. Whether for business meetings, academic lectures, or personal projects, Google Slides offers a wide range of features to make presentations interactive and impactful.

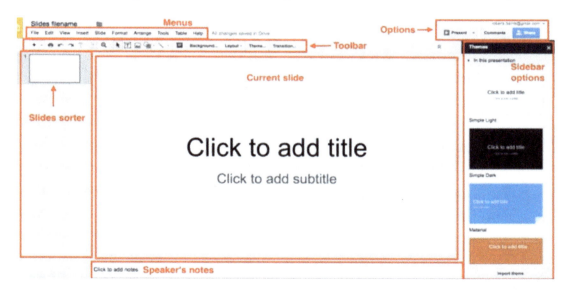

Creating a New Presentation from Scratch

Starting a new Google Slides project is simple and intuitive.

Steps to Create a New Presentation:

1. Open Google Slides and click **Blank Presentation** or choose a template.
2. Rename your presentation by clicking **Untitled Presentation** at the top.

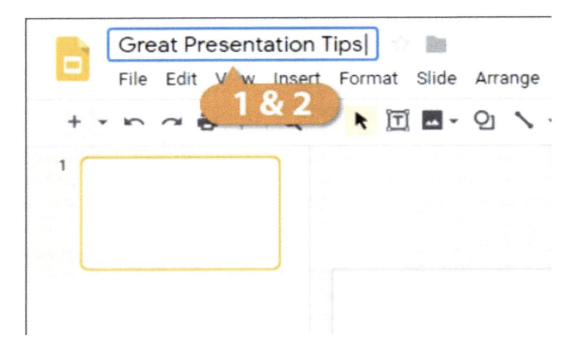

3. Select a **theme** to give your slides a cohesive design.

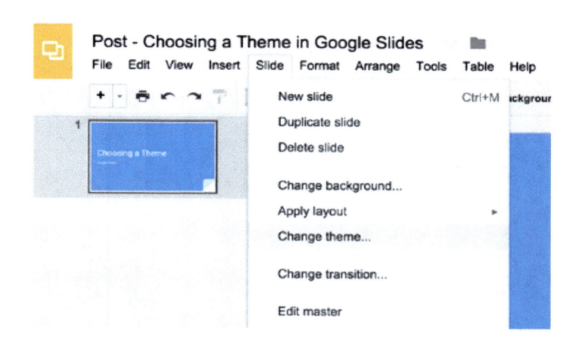

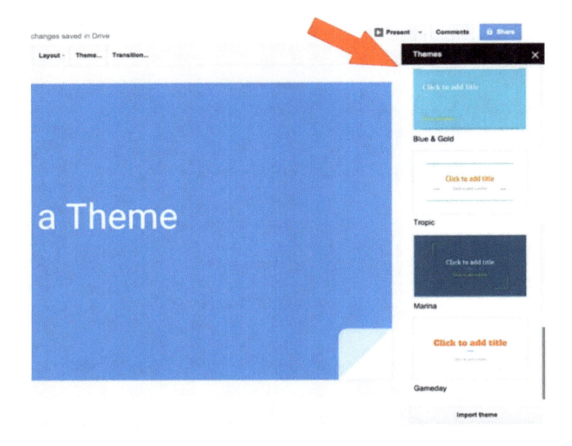

4. Use **Slide > New Slide** or press Ctrl + M to add slides as needed.

💡 **Tip:** Use **template galleries** to speed up the design process with professional layouts.

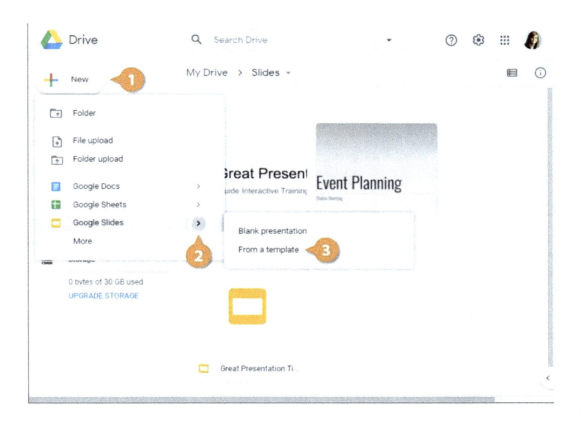

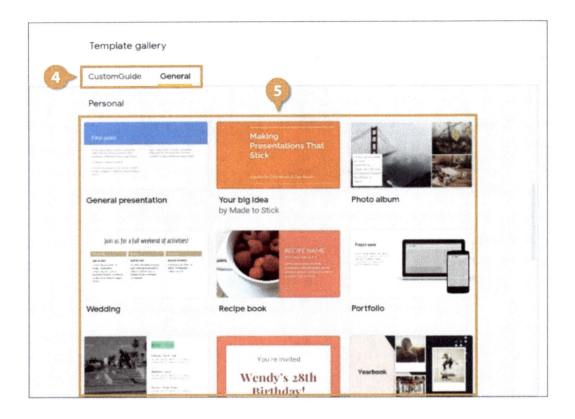

Adding & Formatting Text, Images, and Videos

A well-structured slide includes a mix of text, visuals, and multimedia elements.

Adding & Formatting Text:

- Click on a text box and type your content.
- Customize fonts, colors, and alignments using the **toolbar options**.
- Use **bullets and numbering** (Format > Bullets & Numbering) for structured content.

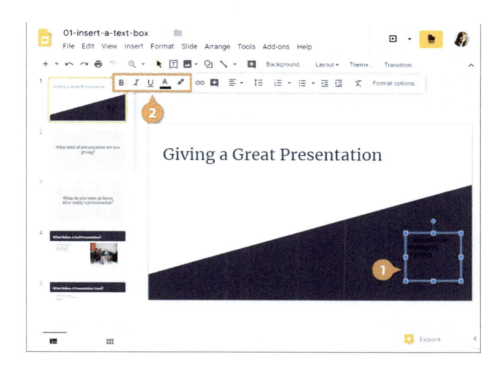

Inserting Images & Videos:

- Go to **Insert > Image** to upload pictures from your device, Google Drive, or the web.

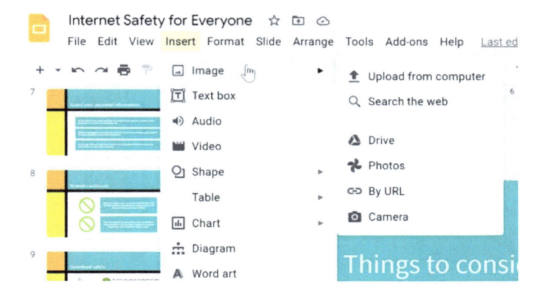

- Select **Insert > Video** to add YouTube clips or upload custom videos.

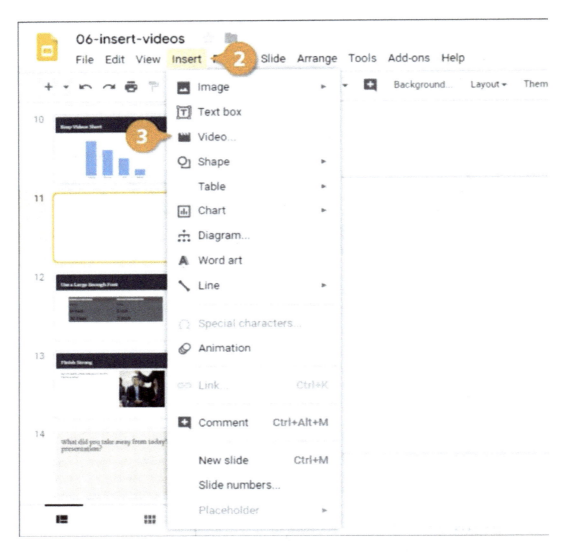

- Resize and reposition elements using drag-and-drop functionality.

💡 **Tip:** Use **alt text** (Right-click > Alt text) on images for accessibility and SEO benefits.

Applying Slide Transitions & Animations

Animations and transitions add visual appeal to presentations.

Adding Slide Transitions:

1. Click on a slide.
2. Go to **Slide > Transition**.

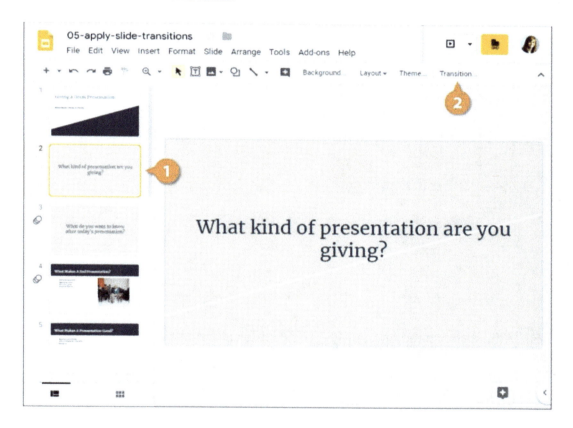

3. Choose an effect (e.g., fade, slide, flip).

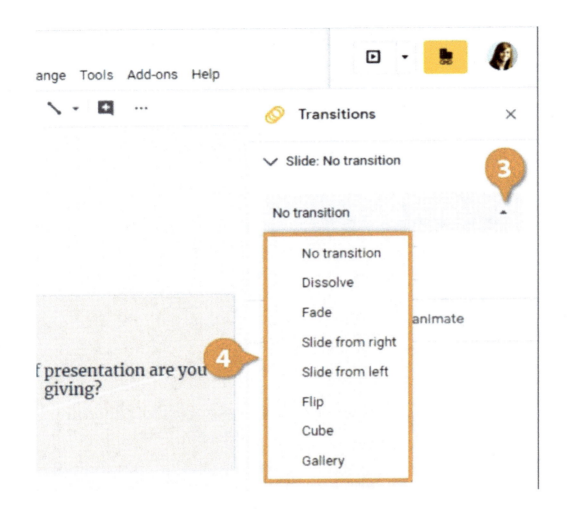

4. Adjust the speed and apply it to all slides if needed.

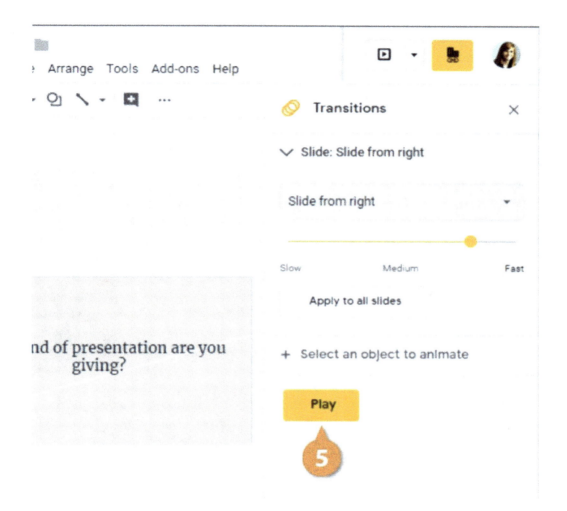

Using Animations for Elements:

1. Select text or an image.
2. Click **Insert > Animation**.

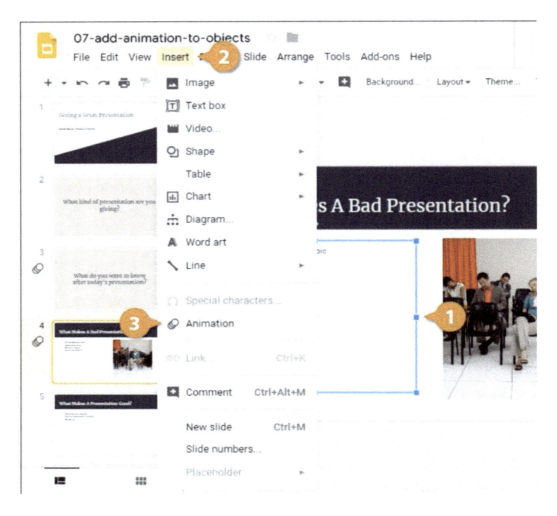

3. Choose an entrance, exit, or emphasis effect.
4. Adjust the **trigger settings** (e.g., **On click, After previous, With previous**).

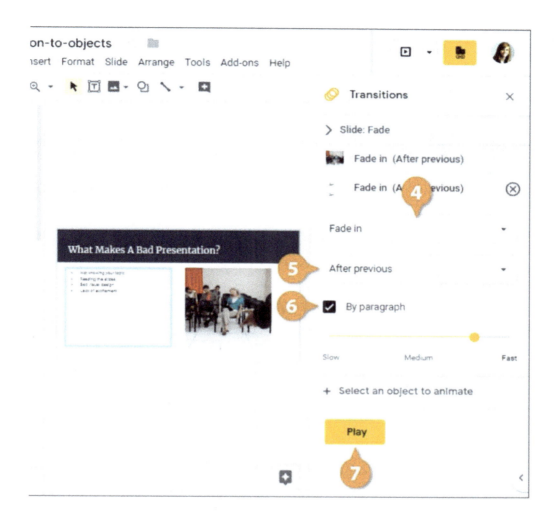

💡 **Tip:** Avoid overloading slides with too many animations, as it can distract from the key message.

Presenting with Speaker Notes

Speaker notes help presenters stay on track without overcrowding slides with text.

How to Use Speaker Notes:

- Click **View > Show Speaker Notes** to enable the notes section.
- Type reminders or additional talking points beneath each slide.

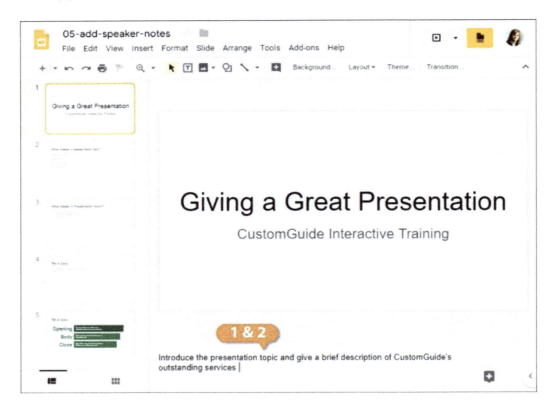

- During the presentation, press Ctrl + Shift + F5 to enter **Presenter View**, where notes are visible only to the speaker.

💡 **Tip:** Print speaker notes (File > Print Settings and Preview > 1 slide with notes) for reference during offline presentations.

Conclusion

Google Slides is a powerful tool for creating professional and engaging presentations. By utilizing text, images, animations, and speaker notes effectively, you can enhance audience engagement and deliver impactful messages.

PART 4: Time & Task Management

Chapter 11: Google Calendar – Organizing Your Schedule Effectively

Google Calendar is a powerful scheduling tool designed to help individuals and teams plan their days, manage events, and stay on top of important tasks. With features like event scheduling, reminders, and integration with other Google services, it serves as a central hub for time management.

Creating & Scheduling Events

Setting up events in Google Calendar ensures you never miss important meetings, appointments, or deadlines.

Steps to Create an Event:

1. Open Google Calendar.
2. Click the **+ Create** button or tap on the desired date and time.

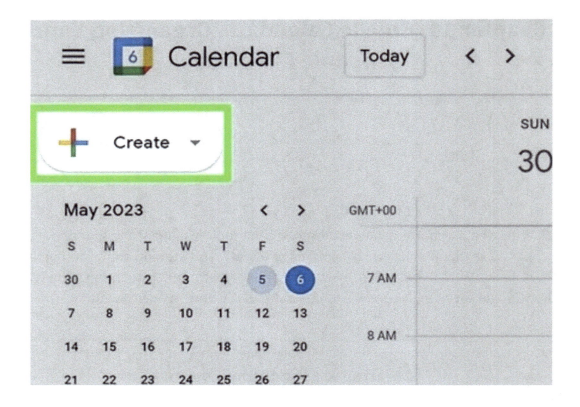

3. Enter an **event title** and specify the **date & time**.

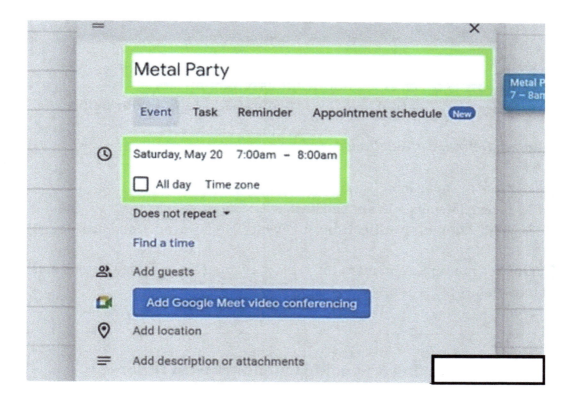

4. Select a location (optional) and add a **Google Meet link** for virtual meetings.
5. Set up a notification to receive reminders before the event.
6. Click **Save** to finalize.

💡 **Tip:** Use **"Find a time"** (available in Google Workspace) to schedule meetings with team members without conflicts.

Setting Up Reminders & Notifications

Google Calendar allows you to configure reminders to ensure you never miss an event.

How to Add Event Reminders:

- While creating or editing an event, go to **Add Notification**.
- Choose between **email notifications** or **pop-up alerts**.
- Select the preferred time (e.g., **10 minutes before, 1 hour before**).

Enabling Default Notifications:

1. Click the **gear icon** (⚙) in the top-right corner.
2. Select **Settings > Event settings**.
3. Adjust **default notifications** for events, all-day events, and tasks.

💡 **Tip:** Set multiple reminders for critical events (e.g., one day before and 15 minutes before).

Sharing & Syncing Calendars with Others

Google Calendar makes collaboration seamless by allowing you to share calendars with colleagues, friends, or family members.

Sharing Your Calendar:

1. In Google Calendar, go to **Settings > My Calendars**.
2. Select the calendar you want to share.

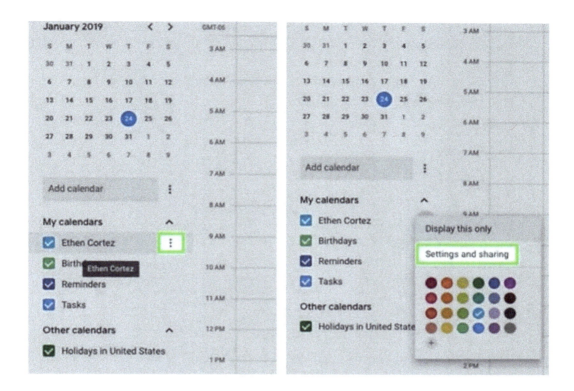

3. Click **Share with specific people** and enter their email addresses.

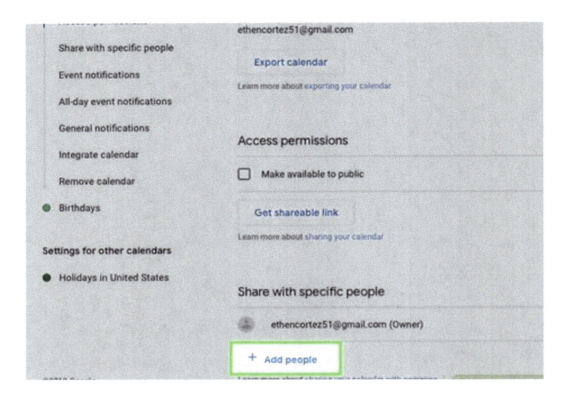

4. Assign permissions (View only, Edit, or Manage).
5. Click **Send** to notify recipients.

Syncing Across Devices:

- Google Calendar syncs automatically with Android and iOS devices.
- To enable syncing on mobile, go to **Settings > Accounts > Google** and ensure Calendar is toggled ON.
- Use **Google Calendar Add-ons** for integration with external apps like Trello, Asana, or Slack.

💡 **Tip:** Create a **shared team calendar** to manage projects, deadlines, and company-wide events efficiently.

Using Google Calendar with Gmail & Google Meet

Google Calendar integrates smoothly with Gmail and Google Meet to simplify scheduling.

Scheduling Events from Gmail:

- Open an email in Gmail and click the **More (⎘) menu > Create event**.
- Google Calendar will auto-fill the event details based on the email content.
- Adjust the time, add participants, and save.

Setting Up Google Meet from Calendar:

- When creating an event, click **Add Google Meet video conferencing**.
- The meeting link is automatically generated and sent to attendees.
- During the event, simply click the **Join with Google Meet** button.

💡 **Tip:** Enable **Focus Time** in Google Calendar to block out distractions and set aside time for deep work.

Conclusion

Google Calendar is more than just a date-tracking tool—it's a complete scheduling solution for individuals and teams. By mastering event creation, reminders, calendar sharing, and integrations, you can optimize your time and improve productivity.

Chapter 12: Google Keep – Capturing & Organizing Your Ideas

Google Keep is a versatile note-taking tool that allows users to jot down thoughts, create checklists, and set reminders—all while seamlessly syncing across devices. Whether you're brainstorming ideas, managing to-do lists, or saving quick notes, Google Keep makes organization effortless.

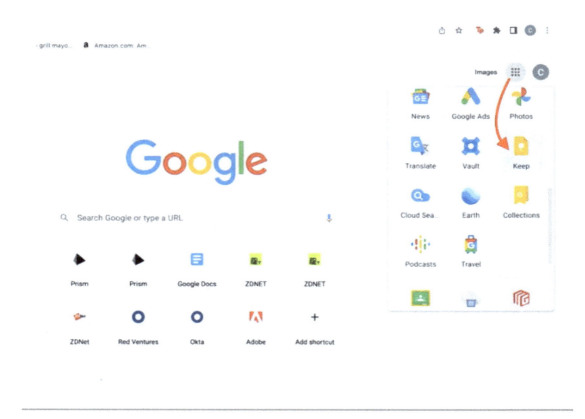

Creating & Formatting Notes

Google Keep provides multiple ways to create and customize notes, making it a flexible tool for personal and professional use.

Steps to Create a New Note:

1. Open Google Keep.
2. Click **Take a note...** at the top.

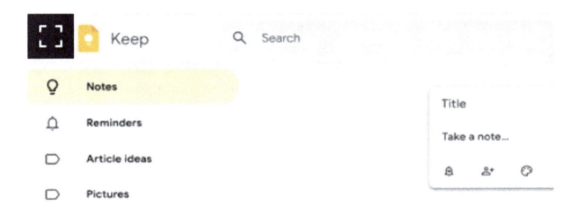

3. Type your content or choose **list mode** for checklists.
4. Add images, drawings, or voice recordings if needed.
5. Click **Close** to save—the note is automatically stored.

Customizing Notes:

- **Pin important notes** to keep them at the top.
- **Use bullet points or checkboxes** for structured lists.
- **Convert handwritten notes** into text using Google Keep's handwriting recognition.

💡 **Tip:** Drag and drop notes to rearrange them in the preferred order.

Using Labels & Color Codes for Organization

Google Keep allows you to categorize notes using labels and colors, making it easy to locate information quickly.

Adding Labels:

1. Open a note and click the, select the **More** (three vertical dots)
2. Select **Add label** and enter a category name (e.g., "Work," "Shopping," "Ideas").

3. Click **Apply**—you can later filter notes by labels for quick access.

Color-Coding Notes:

1. Open a note and click the **Color palette icon**.
2. Choose a color (e.g., **blue for work tasks, yellow for reminders, red for urgent notes**).

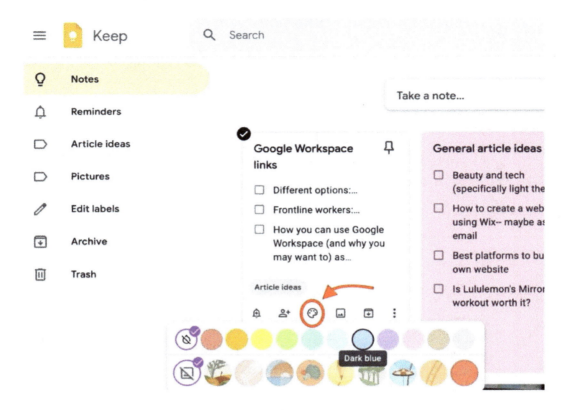

💡 **Tip:** Use **labels + color codes** for a highly organized note-taking system (e.g., all "Work" notes in blue, "Personal" notes in green).

Setting Reminders & Syncing Across Devices

Google Keep integrates reminders to help you stay on track with important tasks.

How to Set Reminders:

1. Open a note and click the **Remind me** (bell) icon.

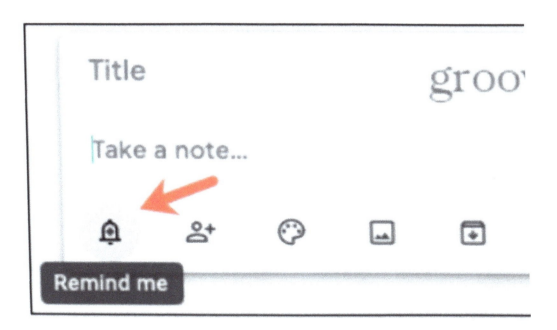

2. Choose a preset time or select **Pick date & time** for custom reminders.
3. For location-based reminders, click **Pick place** and enter a location.
4. Click **Save**—you'll receive notifications when the reminder is due.

Syncing Across Devices:

- Google Keep syncs automatically across **desktop, Android, and iOS devices** when connected to a Google account.
- Notes are accessible via **Google Keep app** or **Google Keep Chrome extension**.

💡 **Tip:** Enable Google Assistant to create notes hands-free by saying, *"Hey Google, take a note."*

Conclusion

Google Keep is an excellent tool for note-taking, idea organization, and task management. By leveraging its features—such as labels, color coding, and reminders—you can stay organized and boost productivity effortlessly.

Chapter 13: Google Tasks – Simplify Your To-Do Lists

Google Tasks is a lightweight yet powerful task management tool integrated with Gmail and Google Calendar. It helps users create, organize, and track to-do lists effortlessly, ensuring productivity without the need for complex task management apps.

Creating Tasks & Subtasks

Google Tasks allows you to break down projects into manageable steps using tasks and subtasks.

Steps to Create a New Task:

1. Open Google Tasks or access it via the **Google Tasks sidebar** in Gmail or Google Calendar.

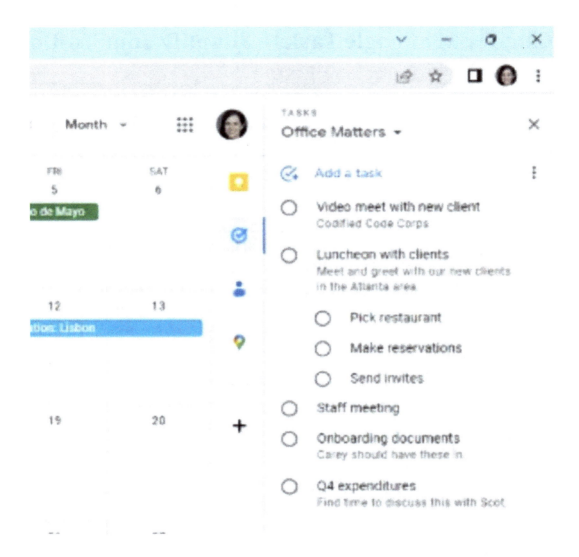

2. Click **"Add a task"** and enter the task description.

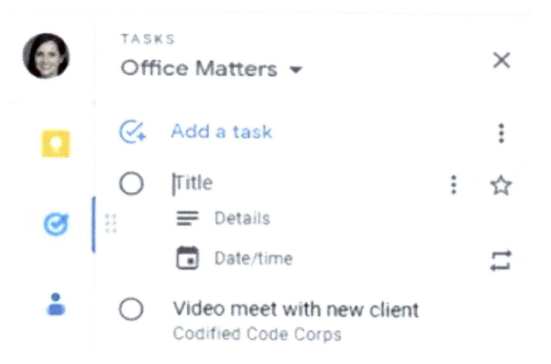

3. Press **Enter** to save the task.

Adding Subtasks:

1. Click on an existing task.
2. Select **"Add a subtask"** and enter the details.

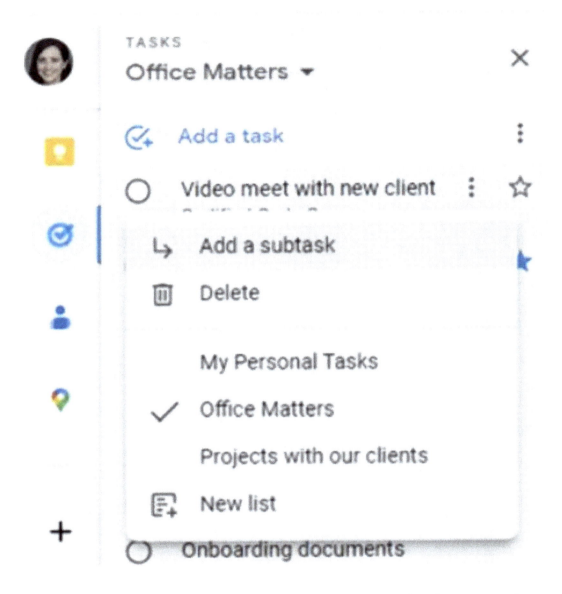

3. Press **Enter** to save—it will now appear nested under the main task.

💡 **Tip:** Use subtasks to break down larger projects into smaller, actionable steps for better organization.

Integrating Tasks with Gmail & Google Calendar

Google Tasks syncs seamlessly with Gmail and Google Calendar, helping you stay on top of deadlines.

Using Tasks in Gmail:

- Open Gmail and click the **Google Tasks icon** in the right sidebar.
- Drag and drop emails into Tasks to automatically create tasks based on emails.
- Click on a task to view the linked email.

Syncing Tasks with Google Calendar:

- Open Google Calendar and check the **Tasks** box under "My Calendars."
- Tasks with due dates will appear in the calendar view.
- Click on a task to edit details or mark it as complete.

💡 **Tip:** Enable notifications in Google Calendar to receive reminders for upcoming tasks.

Setting Deadlines & Reminders

Adding deadlines and reminders helps ensure that important tasks don't get overlooked.

How to Set Due Dates:

1. Click on a task and select the **Calendar icon**.
2. Choose a due date and optional time.
3. The task will now appear in Google Calendar.

Enabling Task Notifications:

- Google Tasks doesn't have built-in reminders, but you can create calendar notifications for tasks with due dates.
- For urgent reminders, consider using **Google Keep** or **Google Assistant** alongside Tasks.

💡 **Tip:** Mark completed tasks to keep track of progress—completed tasks are archived but can be restored if needed.

Conclusion

Google Tasks is an intuitive tool for managing personal and professional to-do lists. By integrating it with Gmail and Google Calendar, setting due dates, and organizing tasks into subtasks, you can streamline your workflow and boost productivity.

PART 5: Business & Team Tools

Chapter 14: Google Sites – Build Websites with Ease

Google Sites is a user-friendly website builder that allows individuals and businesses to create professional-looking websites without any coding knowledge. Whether you need an internal company portal, a project site, or a public-facing website, Google Sites makes the process simple and efficient.

Creating a Website Using Google Sites

Setting up a website with Google Sites is quick and intuitive.

Steps to Create a New Site:

1. Go to [Google Sites](#).
2. Click **Blank** or choose a template from the gallery.

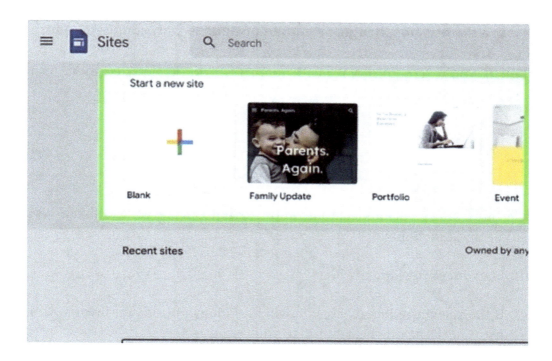

3. Add a **site name** and enter a **title** for the homepage.

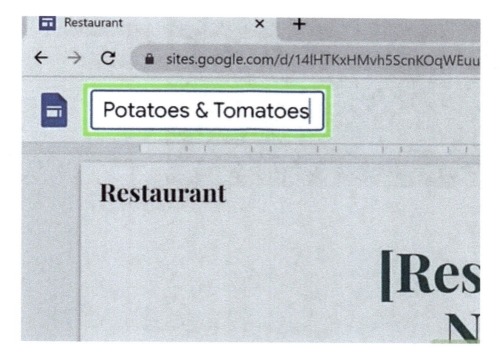

4. Use the **text box, image, or embed options** to start adding content.

💡 **Tip:** If you're creating a website for a team or project, consider using a structured template for consistency and faster setup.

Customizing Layouts & Adding Pages

Google Sites offers various customization tools to make your website visually appealing and functional.

Editing Layout & Design:

- If the select the Insert tab, you will find many options for layouts you can use. Check the one best suited to you.

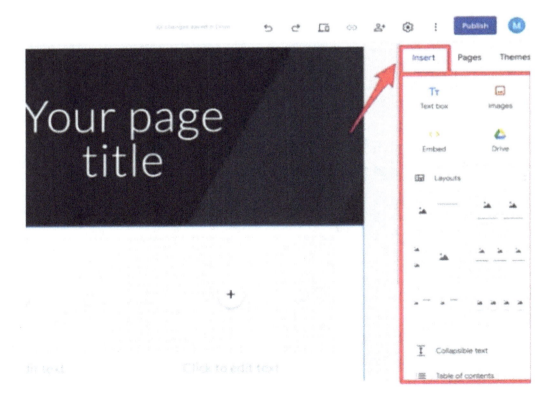

- Use the **Themes tab** to select a color scheme and font style.
- Drag and drop elements to adjust the layout.
- Add **headers, images, videos, buttons, and Google Drive files** for a richer experience.

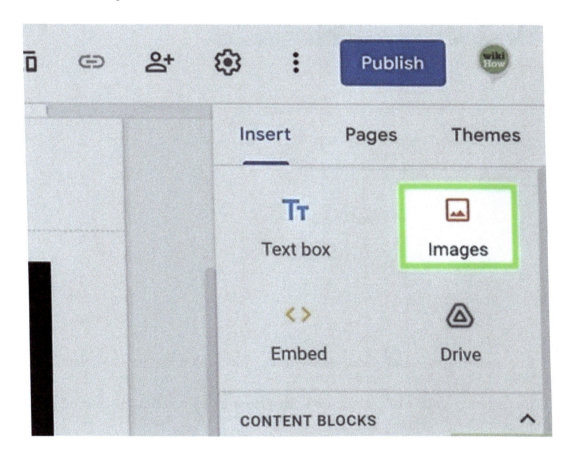

Adding Pages to Your Site:

1. Click **Pages** on the right panel.
2. Select the **+ button** and choose **New page**.

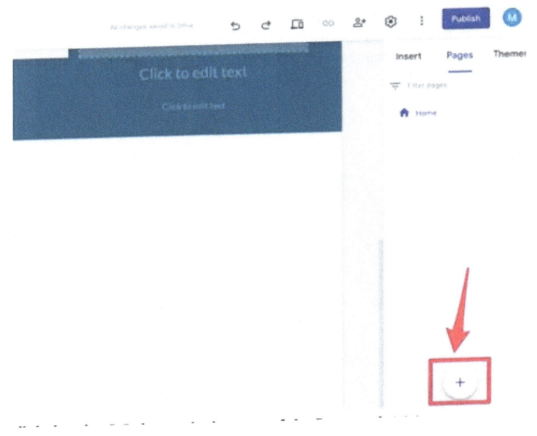

3. Name the page and click **Done**—it will now appear in the site's navigation.

💡 **Tip:** Organize your site's structure with a clear menu by creating **nested pages** (subpages) for better navigation.

Publishing & Managing Permissions

Once your site is ready, you can publish it and manage access settings.

How to Publish Your Site:

1. Preview the site you have created first. Select the Preview icon.

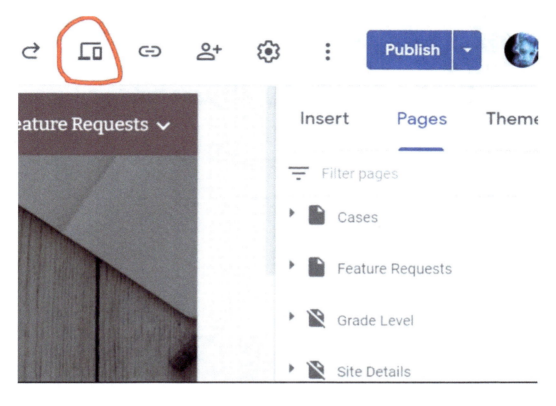

2. Click **Publish** in the top-right corner.
3. Choose a **web address** (e.g., sites.google.com/view/your-site-name).

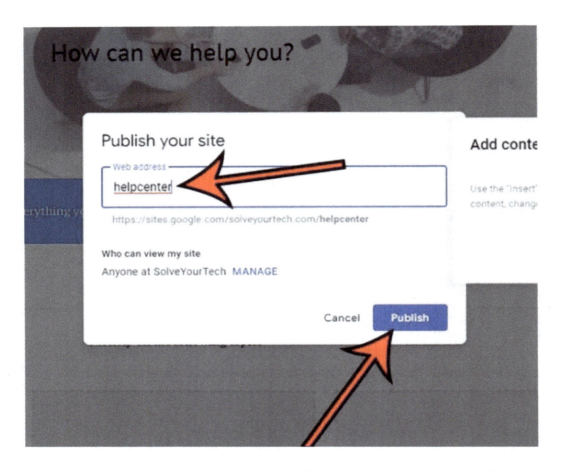

4. Adjust visibility settings—choose **public** or **restricted to specific users**.
5. Click **Publish** to make the site live.

Managing Permissions & Collaboration:

- Click **Share** icon in the top-right corner.

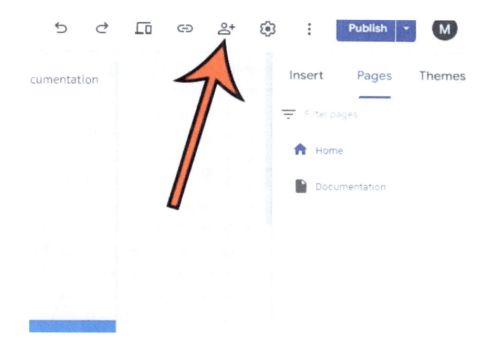

- Add team members with **View or Edit permissions**.

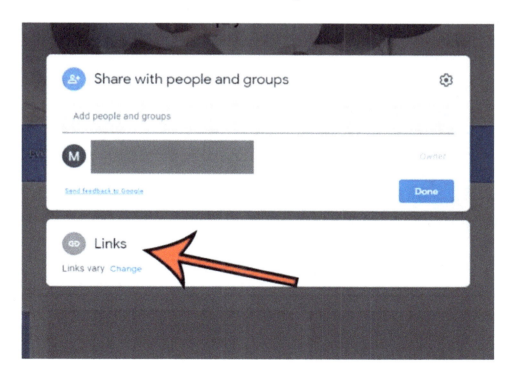

- Control access levels, ensuring only authorized users can make changes.

💡 **Tip:** If you're building an internal website, restrict access to your organization to keep content private.

Conclusion

Google Sites is a powerful tool for creating websites without technical expertise. With its drag-and-drop interface, easy customization options, and seamless integration with Google Drive, you can build and manage websites effortlessly. Whether for business, education, or personal projects, Google Sites provides an accessible solution for everyone.

Chapter 15: Google Admin Console – Managing Your Google Workspace for Business

The **Google Admin Console** is a powerful tool for organizations using Google Workspace. It allows administrators to manage users, set permissions, ensure security, and maintain compliance across all Google Workspace services. Whether you're managing a small team or an enterprise-level organization, the Admin Console is the hub for all administrative tasks.

Adding & Managing Users

Managing users is one of the primary responsibilities of an administrator. The Admin Console allows you to add new users, edit existing profiles, and remove users when needed.

Steps for Adding Users:

1. **Navigate to the Admin Console.**
2. Click on **Users** and then the **Add a user** button.

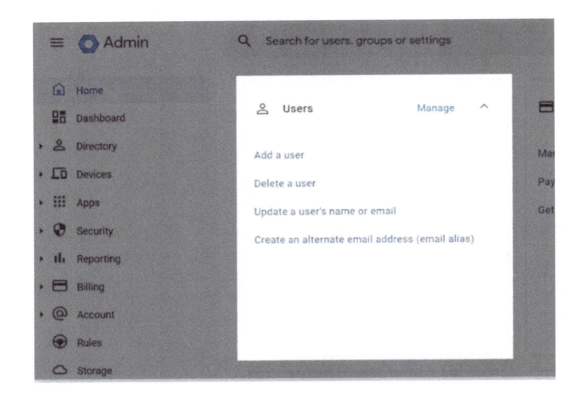

3. Enter the **user's details**, including email, name, and role.
4. **Assign appropriate licenses** for the user's role and responsibilities.
5. Once added, you can **manage user settings**, such as resetting passwords or enabling services.

💡 **Tip:** You can also **bulk upload users** using a CSV file for larger organizations to save time.

Assigning Roles & Permissions

Roles and permissions control what users can access and what they can modify within Google Workspace. Admins can assign predefined roles or create custom ones to fine-tune permissions.

Predefined Roles:

- **Super Admin** – Full access to all settings and data.
- **Groups Admin** – Can manage groups and settings related to them.
- **User Management Admin** – Can add, modify, and delete users but cannot access billing or service settings.

Custom Roles:

You can create **custom roles** for employees, limiting their access to specific areas based on their responsibilities, such as:

- **Email settings only**
- **Calendar and Drive management**
- **Security settings**

💡 **Tip:** Regularly review and update roles and permissions, especially for new hires or those changing departments, to ensure access control aligns with their job functions.

Monitoring Security & Compliance

The Admin Console provides tools to help ensure your organization's security and compliance with internal policies and external regulations. Admins can track user activities, set security alerts, and enforce security policies.

Key Security Features:

- **Two-Factor Authentication (2FA)**: Enforcing 2FA adds an extra layer of protection for all users.
- **Security Reports**: Monitor login attempts, suspicious activity, and unauthorized access.
- **Audit Logs**: Review audit logs to track actions performed by users and identify potential security issues.

- **Compliance Reports**: Ensure that the organization meets compliance requirements by generating detailed reports on security and privacy practices.

💡 **Tip:** Set up automatic **security alerts** to notify admins about any unusual activities, such as login attempts from unfamiliar locations.

Conclusion

The Google Admin Console is an essential tool for managing Google Workspace for business, allowing admins to control user access, permissions, and security settings. By mastering the Admin Console, you can streamline operations, maintain security, and ensure that your organization is compliant with necessary regulations.

Make sure to regularly monitor user activities, review security policies, and adjust settings as your business evolves.

PART 6: Automation & Advanced Features

Chapter 16: Google Apps Script – Automating Google Workspace Tasks

Google Apps Script is a powerful scripting tool that enables you to automate tasks and extend the functionality of Google Workspace. It allows you to create custom workflows, automate repetitive tasks, and even integrate with third-party applications. Whether you're looking to save time, reduce human error, or streamline processes, learning Google Apps Script can drastically enhance your productivity in Google Workspace.

Introduction to Google Apps Script

Google Apps Script is based on JavaScript and runs in the cloud, allowing you to create scripts that interact with Google Workspace tools such as **Google Sheets**, **Google Docs**, **Gmail**, and more. These scripts can be used to automate manual tasks, create custom workflows, and even build standalone applications within Google Workspace.

Key Features:

- **Automate Repetitive Tasks**: Tasks like sending emails, organizing files, and managing calendars can all be automated.
- **Integrate with Google Services**: Scripts can pull and push data from various Google services such as Google Drive, Google Sheets, and Google Calendar.
- **Custom Triggers**: Set up triggers to automatically run scripts on specific events (e.g., time-based triggers or when a file is edited).

💡 **Tip:** Google Apps Script is extremely flexible and can be used for everything from small time-saving hacks to full-fledged automation solutions for your business.

Writing Basic Scripts to Automate Tasks

Writing your first script is easier than you might think. Below is an example of a simple script that sends a daily reminder email.

Steps to Write a Basic Script:

1. **Open Google Sheets** (or any other Google app).
2. Go to **Extensions > Apps Script**.

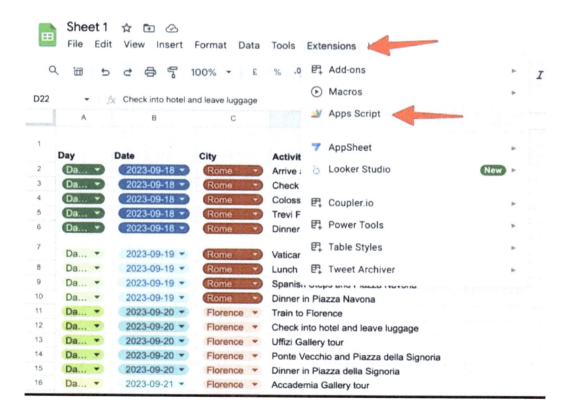

3. In the Apps Script editor, start writing your script. For example:

```
function sendReminder() {
  var emailAddress = "your-email@example.com";
  var subject = "Daily Reminder";
  var message = "This is your daily reminder to complete your task.";

  MailApp.sendEmail(emailAddress, subject, message);
}
```

4. **Save** the script and then set a trigger:
   - Go to **Triggers** and select **Time-driven trigger**.
   - Choose how often you want the script to run, such as once a day.

💡 **Tip:** Start with small scripts to automate simple tasks and gradually build your knowledge to tackle more complex workflows.

Creating Custom Google Docs & Sheets Add-ons

One of the most powerful uses of Google Apps Script is creating custom add-ons for Google Docs or Sheets. Add-ons can enhance the functionality of your documents or spreadsheets, making them more efficient for your specific needs.

Steps to Create a Google Sheets Add-on:

1. Open **Google Sheets** and go to **Extensions > Apps Script**.
2. Write a script for your custom functionality. For example, create a function that formats a sheet based on specific criteria.

```
function formatSheet() {
  var sheet = SpreadsheetApp.getActiveSpreadsheet().getActiveSheet();
  sheet.getRange("A1:B1").setBackground("yellow").setFontWeight("bold");
}
```

3. To publish your script as an add-on, select **Publish > Deploy from Manifest** and follow the steps to make it available for others to use (optional).

Creating a Google Docs Add-on:

- Similarly, you can create add-ons for Google Docs by scripting custom features such as inserting standard templates, formatting documents, or inserting images automatically.

💡 **Tip:** Once you've created your add-on, you can share it with your team or even publish it in the **Google Workspace Marketplace**.

Conclusion

Google Apps Script is an invaluable tool for automating tasks and enhancing the functionality of Google Workspace. By learning the basics of Apps Script, you can automate mundane tasks, create custom add-ons, and build powerful workflows that streamline your operations.

Once you're comfortable with the basics, dive deeper into creating custom scripts, setting up triggers, and integrating Google services to truly unlock the full potential of Google Workspace.

Chapter 17: Google Workspace Integrations & Enhancing Productivity with Third-Party Apps

Google Workspace offers a wide range of tools that seamlessly integrate with third-party applications to boost productivity and streamline workflows. By connecting Google Workspace with other services like Zapier, Slack, Trello, Asana, and Chrome extensions, you can take your workspace to the next level. This chapter will guide you through the most powerful integrations and how they can enhance your Google Workspace experience.

Connecting Google Workspace with Zapier

Zapier is a powerful automation tool that allows you to connect Google Workspace with thousands of third-party apps. With **Zapier**, you can automate tasks between apps, saving you valuable time and reducing the need for manual input.

Popular Automations for Google Workspace:

- **Gmail & Trello**: Automatically create Trello cards from new Gmail emails with specific labels or keywords.
- **Google Sheets & Slack**: Set up a workflow to post a Slack message when new data is added to a Google Sheet.
- **Google Drive & Dropbox**: Automatically move files from Google Drive to Dropbox for backup.

How to Set Up Zapier with Google Workspace:

1. Sign up for a **Zapier** account.
2. Choose Google Workspace and the third-party app you wish to integrate.
3. Follow the steps to authenticate your Google account.
4. Set the conditions and actions that define your "Zap" (automated workflow).

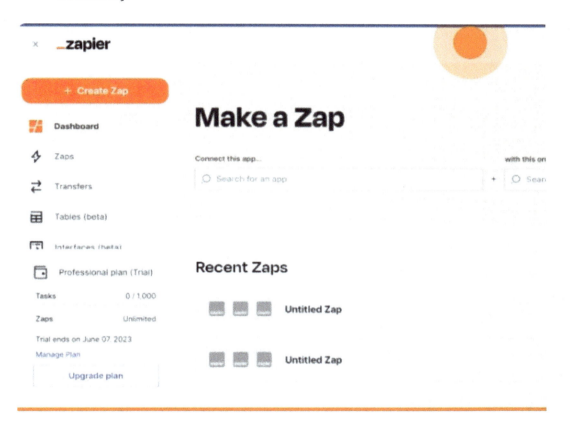

*Select **Create Zap***

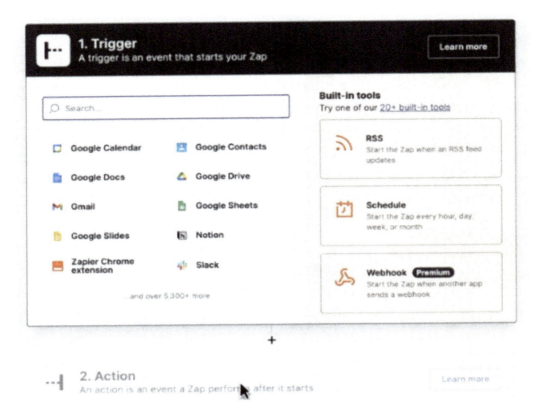

Choose the trigger event (any of the workspace tools you want to integrate)

5. Test the Zap to ensure it's functioning correctly.

💡 **Tip:** Zapier is great for automating repetitive tasks and integrating Google Workspace with apps you already use daily. Start with simple automations and gradually scale as you get more comfortable.

Using Google Workspace with Slack, Trello & Asana

Google Workspace integrates seamlessly with popular team collaboration tools like **Slack**, **Trello**, and **Asana**. These tools can enhance communication, project management, and collaboration across teams, all while keeping everything connected with Google Workspace.

Slack & Google Workspace:

Slack is a messaging platform that can be connected with Google Workspace to keep all team communications and documents in one place.

- **Gmail Integration**: Receive notifications from Gmail directly in Slack and even send emails from Slack.
- **Google Drive Integration**: Share Google Docs, Sheets, and Slides files directly within Slack channels. You can even preview the documents within Slack.

Trello & Google Workspace:

Trello is a project management tool that integrates perfectly with Google Workspace to streamline task management.

- **Gmail to Trello**: Convert emails into Trello cards by forwarding them to a designated Trello board.
- **Google Drive & Trello**: Attach Google Drive files to your Trello cards, making it easy to keep your documents and tasks in sync.

Asana & Google Workspace:

Asana is another excellent project management tool, and integrating it with Google Workspace can help you stay on top of tasks.

- **Google Calendar & Asana**: Sync tasks with Google Calendar to stay updated on deadlines and milestones.
- **Google Drive & Asana**: Attach files from Google Drive to Asana tasks, ensuring all necessary documents are right where you need them.

💡 **Tip:** Integration with tools like Slack, Trello, and Asana allows you to centralize communication, file-sharing, and project tracking, making team collaboration smoother and more efficient.

Enhancing Productivity with Chrome Extensions

Google Chrome extensions can enhance your productivity by adding valuable features directly to your browser. Many extensions are specifically designed to work with Google Workspace, making it even easier to manage tasks and integrate third-party tools.

Useful Chrome Extensions for Google Workspace:

- **Grammarly**: This extension helps you write error-free emails and documents in Gmail, Google Docs, and other Google Workspace tools.
- **Google Keep Chrome Extension**: Quickly add notes to Google Keep from any webpage and access your notes across devices.
- **Trello Extension**: Create Trello cards directly from Google Docs or Gmail with the Trello Chrome extension.
- **Google Drive File Stream**: Easily access and manage Google Drive files from your computer's file system without taking up local storage.

How to Install Chrome Extensions:

1. Open the **Chrome Web Store**.
2. Search for the extension you want (e.g., "Grammarly" or "Trello").
3. Click **Add to Chrome**.
4. Follow the prompts to complete the installation.
5. Access and configure the extension from the Chrome toolbar.

💡 **Tip:** Chrome extensions can drastically reduce the time it takes to complete tasks by adding one-click solutions and streamlining your workflow.

Conclusion

By integrating Google Workspace with tools like **Zapier**, **Slack**, **Trello**, **Asana**, and utilizing **Chrome extensions**, you can dramatically improve your productivity. These integrations enable automation, enhance team collaboration, and streamline workflows, helping you achieve more in less time. Take advantage of these powerful tools to unlock the full potential of Google Workspace and maximize your efficiency.

PART 7: Troubleshooting & Expert Tips

Chapter 18: Troubleshooting Common Google Workspace Issues & Solutions

---

W hile Google Workspace is designed to offer seamless integration across various tools, occasional issues may arise. Whether it's recovering lost files, resolving sync errors, or fixing Google Meet connectivity problems, understanding how to troubleshoot these challenges will help you maintain productivity. This chapter will guide you through some common issues you may encounter and provide practical solutions to resolve them.

Recovering Lost Files & Restoring Deleted Emails

One of the most frustrating situations is accidentally losing important files or emails. Fortunately, Google Workspace offers several ways to recover lost data, ensuring you can retrieve documents and emails with minimal hassle.

Recovering Files in Google Drive:

Google Drive offers a built-in **Trash** folder where deleted files are temporarily stored for up to 30 days.

1. Open **Google Drive** and click on **Trash** in the left-hand sidebar.
2. Locate the file you want to restore and right-click it.
3. Select **Restore** to move the file back to its original location.

If the file was permanently deleted or removed from Trash:

- **Google Drive Version History**: If you can't find the file, use the **Version History** feature. Right-click on the folder that housed the missing file and select **Manage Versions** to view and restore older versions.

Restoring Deleted Emails in Gmail:

If you've accidentally deleted an email, Gmail provides a way to recover it within 30 days:

1. Open Gmail and click on the **Trash** folder.
2. Find the email you want to recover and click on it.
3. Click the **Move to** icon and choose **Inbox** or another folder to restore the email.

If it's no longer in Trash, you can attempt to recover emails from Gmail's **Mail Recovery Tool**:

1. Go to Gmail's **Help** section and search for the "**Recover deleted messages**" option.
2. Follow the instructions to request a recovery.

💡 **Tip:** Regularly back up important files and emails to prevent accidental loss. Use **Google Vault** if you're on a business plan, as it allows for extended retention and recovery of data.

Fixing Sync Issues with Google Drive & Calendar

Sync issues can be disruptive, especially when you're unable to access or update files and calendar events across devices. Here's how to resolve common sync problems:

Google Drive Sync Issues:

1. **Check Your Internet Connection**: Ensure your device is connected to a stable internet connection. Slow or intermittent connectivity can cause syncing delays.
2. **Clear Cache**: If Google Drive isn't syncing, try clearing your browser or app cache.
   - **On Desktop**: Open Chrome and go to **Settings > Privacy and security > Clear browsing data**.
   - **On Mobile**: Go to **Settings > Apps > Google Drive** and tap **Clear Cache**.
3. **Reauthorize Google Drive**: If syncing persists, sign out of your Google account and sign back in to reauthorize Google Drive.

Google Calendar Sync Issues:

If your Google Calendar is not syncing correctly, follow these troubleshooting steps:

1. **Refresh the Calendar**: Sometimes a simple refresh can resolve syncing issues. Click the **Refresh** button on the Calendar webpage.
2. **Check Google Calendar App**: If you're using a mobile device, ensure that **Calendar sync** is enabled in your settings.
   - On Android: Go to **Settings > Accounts > Google > Sync Calendar**.
   - On iPhone: Open **Settings > Mail > Accounts > Google** and enable Calendar sync.
3. **Clear App Cache**: If syncing is still not working, clear the Google Calendar app's cache (on mobile devices) or browser cache (on desktops).

💡 **Tip:** Ensure your Google apps are up-to-date to avoid sync issues that may arise from outdated software versions.

Resolving Google Meet Connectivity Issues

Google Meet is widely used for video conferencing, but connectivity issues can arise from network problems, browser settings, or incorrect permissions. Here's how to resolve common Google Meet problems:

Troubleshooting Google Meet Connection Issues:

1. **Check Your Internet Speed**: A slow internet connection can cause video and audio problems. For the best experience, ensure your internet speed is at least 3 Mbps for both upload and download.
2. **Clear Cache & Cookies**: Overloaded browser data can slow down Google Meet. Clear your browser's cache and cookies.
3. **Update Your Browser**: Using an outdated browser can cause compatibility issues. Ensure you're using an up-to-date version of Chrome, Firefox, or Edge.
4. **Disable Extensions**: Browser extensions can sometimes interfere with Google Meet. Disable any unnecessary extensions, especially ad blockers or VPNs, which could block meeting features.
5. **Allow Camera & Microphone Permissions**: Ensure that your browser has permission to use your camera and microphone. Go to the browser's settings and allow **Meet** to access these devices.

Troubleshooting Audio/Video Problems:

- **Audio Issues**: If you can't hear others or they can't hear you, check your microphone and speaker settings. Ensure they are configured correctly and not muted.
- **Video Problems**: If your video isn't showing up, check your camera settings and ensure the camera isn't blocked by another app or device.

💡 **Tip:** Always test your Google Meet connection a few minutes before your meeting to troubleshoot any potential issues.

Conclusion

Google Workspace tools are robust and highly reliable, but occasional issues like lost files, sync problems, and video conferencing challenges can arise. By following these troubleshooting steps, you can quickly resolve most problems and get back to work without missing a beat. Regularly checking for software updates, clearing caches, and ensuring proper permissions can prevent many common issues from happening in the first place.

Chapter 19: Unlocking Google Workspace's Hidden Gems

Google Workspace is packed with useful tools that can elevate your productivity, streamline your workflow, and boost your efficiency. Beyond the basic features, there are hidden tips and advanced functions that can make a significant difference in how you use Google Workspace tools. This chapter highlights must-know keyboard shortcuts, free resources, and the latest updates that can take your Google Workspace experience to the next level.

Mastering Keyboard Shortcuts for Enhanced Efficiency

Google Workspace offers an array of keyboard shortcuts that can help you navigate through apps faster, streamline your tasks, and increase overall productivity. Whether you're working in Gmail, Google Docs, or Google Sheets, these shortcuts are valuable tools for working smarter, not harder.

Must-Know Shortcuts for Google Workspace:

1. **Gmail Shortcuts:**
    - **Compose a New Email:** Press **C** to start a new message.
    - **Send Email:** Press **Ctrl + Enter** (Windows) or **Cmd + Enter** (Mac).
    - **Archive Email:** Press **E** to archive the selected email.
    - **Move to Trash:** Press **#** to send an email to Trash.
    - **Search Emails:** Press **/ (forward slash)** to jump to the search bar.
2. **Google Docs Shortcuts:**
    - **Bold Text:** Press **Ctrl + B** (Windows) or **Cmd + B** (Mac).

making email composition quicker and more efficient. It learns from your writing style, adapting to your tone over time.

2. **Google Meet Background Effects:** New background options in Google Meet have been rolled out, allowing you to blur or replace your background with images. This is especially useful for maintaining professionalism during virtual meetings.

3. **Google Sheets Formula Suggestions:** Google Sheets now features **Formula Suggestions**, where it automatically suggests formulas based on the data you are working with. This feature can save you time when performing calculations or working with data sets.

4. **Improved Google Drive Search:** Google Drive's search functionality has been enhanced with the ability to search by **keywords within documents** or **type of file** (e.g., spreadsheets, presentations). You can now also search for files shared with specific people or organizations.

5. **Google Docs Collaboration Improvements:** Google Docs has added **suggestion mode** enhancements, making it easier to accept or reject edits, especially when collaborating on large documents. This is ideal for teams working together on written content.

💡 **Tip:** Subscribe to the **Google Workspace Updates Blog** to get timely information on new features and updates as they are rolled out. You can also enable **automatic updates** for your apps to ensure you never miss the latest features.

Conclusion

By mastering keyboard shortcuts, utilizing free templates, and keeping an eye on the latest updates, you can unlock the full potential of Google Workspace. Whether you're saving time with automation, streamlining collaboration with templates, or enhancing productivity through the latest features, these tools can dramatically improve how you work. Stay ahead by leveraging these hidden gems and continuously evolving your skills in Google Workspace.

Index

www.ingramcontent.com/pod-product-compliance
Lightning Source LLC
LaVergne TN
LVHW081526050326
832903LV00025B/1651